W9-BRP-079

Christmas 2002

An Owner's Guide To

THE GARDEN POND

Howell Book House

Howell Book House
A Simon & Schuster Macmillan Company
1633 Broadway
New York, NY 10019

Macmillan Publishing books may be purchased for business or sales promotional use. For information please write: Special Markets Department, Macmillan Publishing USA, 1633 Broadway, New York, NY 10019.

Library of Congress Cataloging-in-Publication Data
Conrad, Roseanne D.
An owner's guide to the garden pond / by Roseanne D. Conrad.
p. cm.
Includes bibliographical references.
ISBN 0-87605-447-5
1. Water gardens.   I. Title.
SB423.C65   1998
635.9'674—DC21   97-45784
                      CIP

Manufactured in the United States of America
10 9 8 7 6 5 4 3 2

Series Director: Amanda Pisani
Series Assistant Director: Jennifer Liberts
Book Design: Michele Laseau
Cover Design: Iris Jeromnimon
Illustrations: Rod Baldassarre
Photography:
  Cover photo by B. Everett Webb; inset photo by Doug Elliot; back cover photo by Renée Stockdale
  Roseanne D. Conrad: 2–3, 7, 8, 30, 47, 49, 52 (bottom), 59
  Doug Elliot: 40, 123
  Zig Leszczynski: 44, 45, 48, 51, 52 (top), 58, 61, 65, 66, 67, 69, 85, 86, 87, 89, 99, 112, 115, 116
  Courtesy of Little Giant Co.: 34
  Bob Romar: 119
  Renée Stockdale: Title page, 5, 10, 15, 17, 26, 27, 38–39, 46, 54, 76, 78, 82, 90, 106, 108, 109
  John Tyson: 37, 42, 92, 94, 98
  B. Everett Webb: 104, 111
  Gary Wittstock/Pond Supplies of America: 9, 13, 14, 19, 23, 28, 35, 43, 55, 56, 57, 62, 70, 72, 102–103, 118, 121
Production Team: Toi Davis, Natalie Hollifield, Clint Lahnen, Angel Perez, Dennis Sheehan, Terri Sheehan, Chris Van Camp

Contents

Welcome
to the
World

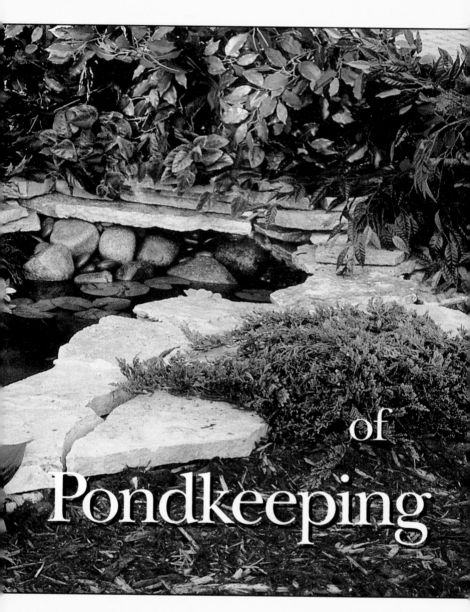

of

Pondkeeping

Features of the Garden Pond

Water Line

Terrace

Slope

Soil

Basin

Marginals

Paving Stones

Ground Surface

Liner

Marginal Plants

chapter 1

Water in Your Garden

Water . . . humans are naturally drawn to it. The slightest trickle captures our attention, imagination and childlike curiosity. We depend upon it for our very survival and we gravitate towards it for our recreational purposes. We tend to  plan our vacations around it, whether it's a trip to the ocean, a mountain lake or a favorite fishing stream. At home, we install swimming pools, hot tubs, fountains and birdbaths. Is it any wonder then that many of us yearn to have a garden pond in our backyard?

Until just a few years ago, a garden pond was, for many, just a dream. They were expensive and time-consuming to install, and quite costly and difficult to maintain. But today, thanks to the wide variety of pond liner materials and water gardening products available, water gardening can be an inexpensive and enjoyable task. Most people are able to install and maintain an ornamental garden pond themselves if they follow some basic guidelines.

This book will serve as a guide for entry-level pond-keepers. It will help you to determine where to install your garden pond and the style and size of pond to suit your particular tastes and situation; it will describe the species of aquatic plants that are recommended and available in your part of the country; it will tell you what kind of pond inhabitants you can safely introduce to your pond, and which ones might come uninvited; it will also give you simple, step-by-step measures for year-round maintenance and upkeep.

Adding a Pond to Your Garden

Most people who long for a garden pond are "gardeners" first. They enjoy spending time out of doors and are always seeking new ways to surround themselves with nature. If you are considering a garden pond, it is safe to assume that you already have a garden and landscaping around your home with established trees, shrubs, flowering plants and some hardscaping, such as a patio or deck. What you will be doing then, is incorporating a pond into what you have already created—another feature to add color and texture to your garden canvas.

A garden pond will serve as a focal point and the finishing touch to your garden. It will magically bring all the elements of your garden together—naturally. It will enhance the features of your garden and will make it appear much larger. The reflective qualities of a garden pond bring in clouds and treetops to rest upon its surface, mesmerizing us as though it were a large gazing globe. A trickling waterfall or splashing fountain will add soothing sounds and movement to your garden.

A garden pond is also a water source for wildlife. You will be amazed at the amount of wildlife that even a small pond will attract. Frogs, toads, dragonflies, butterflies, birds and other small animals will welcome this addition to your garden.

Almost any garden (and certainly all gardeners!) will benefit with the addition of a water garden.

Types of Ponds and Water Gardens

An ornamental garden pond should look natural, as though it was meant to be there—as though it has always been there. Even a newly installed pond can look "established" if it has been installed in the right place and if the design elements complement the existing landscape.

There are two distinct styles of garden ponds: formal and informal. A formal design is symmetrical, such as a circle, square, rectangle, oval or octagon. Formal ponds are often made of cement and usually don't incorporate a lot of plant material either in or around the pond. Uncluttered simplicity and elegance best describe a formal pond.

An informal design is asymmetrical or "free-form." This style can take on the look of a kidney (or crescent), a butterfly or any other free-form object. This style is more like those that you would find in nature. Free-form ponds may also be constructed using cement, but the material of choice for this type of pond is usually a heavy rubber material that conforms to the curves and angles of the pond. This and other material will be discussed later in the book. Informal ponds can easily be incorporated into the garden. Perennial and annual beds can wrap

A formal pond is simple and elegant.

7

around the perimeter of the pond, adding colorful and ever-changing reflections in the water. Decks, landscape timbers, meandering stepping stones and other types of winding pathways, garden benches, landscape mulch, antique hand pumps, troughs and milk cans all work wonderfully when incorporated into a water garden.

Once you have established the style of pond that you would like, you can then decide what design elements you will include, such as waterfalls, streams, fountains and statuary. You will also need to choose the liner material and the coping (or edging) materials that you will use on the perimeter of the pond. Each design element will produce a different effect and will necessitate varying installation considerations.

An informal design has an asymmetrical form.

When designing your pond you might also want to choose a "theme" such as Japanese, Cottage, Heritage and so on. This theme should complement your home and existing garden theme.

Japanese-style gardens (and ponds) are timeless in their beauty, simplicity and mystique. True Japanese-style gardens are purposeful. Every rock laid is symbolic, and every element should accent the garden's relation to nature. In a Japanese garden there are five distinctive styles: hill-and-pond style, tea garden style, stroll style, courtyard style and dry landscape style. Many incorporate two or more styles within their design. Although all five of the styles are different, all focus on a peaceful sense of space away from the busy world where one can reflect, relax and become one with nature. Japanese-style gardening is fascinating and an interesting subject to study. If you wish to design your pond in true Japanese style, there is a wealth of information available in book form and on the Internet. (Hint:

Irises are beautiful in and outside the Japanese garden pond. There are many varieties and colors available to add a splash of spring excitement to your pond.)

*The beauty of a
Japanese-style
garden is timeless.*

Water Gardening in Containers

Apartment dwellers and people with small yards may also yearn for a water garden but may assume that it is beyond their reach. With a little imagination, you can fit a water garden just about anywhere using a container. Pots, tubs, barrels, buckets, basins, bowls, urns, saucers, aquariums, troughs, window boxes . . . if it will hold water, you can water garden in it!

CHOOSING A CONTAINER

Container gardens appeal to just about everyone because of their size and ease of installation and upkeep. You can use most anything as a container, so long as it is nontoxic and free of holes and cracks. Half whiskey barrels are a favorite choice for many people. They are attractive, relatively inexpensive and easy to find. They are large enough and deep enough to hold a variety of aquatic plants as well as a few Goldfish or other small pond fish. Of course, the whiskey barrel will have to be lined, because it can leach toxins into the water. Best choices for lining these barrels are either a 5 foot by 5 foot piece of rubber liner or the very easy preformed "drop-in" liners available from a variety of manufacturers. There are even spillway varieties available, which work wonderfully if you want to stack the barrels with one spilling into another.

Terra-cotta pots are another favorite container, but these need to be sealed before they are used for aquatic plants and fish. Polyurethane or any of the other sealers on the market (so long as they are non-

toxic) will work well. Several coats may need to be applied (with ample drying time allocated between coats) before the pot is completely watertight. If there happens to be a drainage hole in the bottom of the pot, it is easily plugged by first putting a few pieces of tape (gaffers or electrical) over the hole in a crisscross fashion on the outside of the pot. Then, fill the hole with plumber's epoxy. Allow to harden before filling with water, plants and fish.

Of course, there are many containers available in the marketplace created specifically for aquatic purposes.

Stacked barrels provide an engaging waterfall.

Many of these are made of lightweight plastics, which makes them easy to lift and move from place to place. They are also easy to clean and can be used for years.

GROWING PLANTS IN CONTAINER GARDENS

Plants are easily grown in containers. There is nothing more stunning than a Lotus or Water Lily in a painted ceramic basin! Groupings of plants work well in containers, too. Six or seven varieties can share a single whiskey barrel container. For a lush and interesting container water garden, consider a Water Lily (be sure it is a small variety) combined with a Water Hyacinth, a Water Lettuce, a Parrots Feather, Duckweed or Azolla and a tall-growing foliage plant, such as a variegated Sweetflag or a Dwarf Papyrus. The Water Lily pot will be placed in the bottom of the container. You should use a 16-inch round by 7-inch high pot for the Lily. The Sweetflag or tall foliage plant should be placed in a more narrow pot. Bricks can be placed next to the Water Lily pot and the foliage plant can set atop these bricks. The other plants are floating plants, so they do not need to be potted. You will need to divide and remove the floating plants from time to time, as they multiply rapidly, causing crowding problems.

Unless you are located in a freeze-free zone, containers will not overwinter well and most plants will have to be placed in a deeper pond, overwintered indoors or treated as annuals and discarded in the fall.

PUMPS AND FILTERS FOR CONTAINERS

Experts disagree as to whether a container water garden needs a pump and filter. Some feel that you must have a pump to add oxygen to the water and a filter to control the fish waste. I have found that when a tub or container is stocked with a good balance of plants and fish, there is no need for a pump or filter. The plants give off oxygen, and the floating plants keep the water below cool and shaded. This also helps to inhibit algae growth. The fish will eat mosquito larvae and other insects and forage in the plant material and the small amounts of algae that will grow along the

Bricks can be used to support the plants in your container garden.

11

sides of the pots. The fish waste will provide nutrients for the plants. Of course, if you overfeed the fish, you will promote waste buildup, which can lead to an unhealthy ammonia problem.

KEEP THE WATER CLEAN AND FRESH

You will usually not need to make a water change through the summer in a container water garden, providing the container is large and deep enough and is stocked with adequate plant material. You will need to add water as evaporation lowers the level, however. During the heat of the summer, and especially during periods of drought, you may need to top it off every day or two.

You can help to keep the water clear by including a few Goldfish or small pond fish in your container water garden. Without fish, your tub will probably become "buggy"—the water cloudy and stagnant. This cloudiness is a result of the presence of eggs laid by mosquitoes and other insects in the water. The fish remedy this problem by enthusiastically eating the larvae as well as other small insects.

You may wish to hear the sound of splashing or trickling water in your container. There are many spouters on the market that easily attach to the rims of containers. Spouting frogs, turtles, birds and dolphins all make lovely additions to the container water garden. They also help to aerate the water as the water recirculates. A small pump that forces water through a tube and through the spouter is placed in the container. You can wrap the pump loosely with a piece of filter mesh, which can be purchased at most locations that deal in water-gardening products.

PRACTICE WITH A CONTAINER GARDEN

If you're not sure that a backyard pond is right for you, practice with a container garden! This mini-garden gives you the opportunity to experiment with growing a variety of plants and housing a small number of fish before you bring out the shovels. Container gardens are both exceptionally beautiful and exceptionally easy to care for—the perfect choice for the novice gardener.

chapter 2

Choosing
a **Site** for
Your **Pond**

The most important part of installing a pond is selecting the site. You will need to consider many issues when choosing a location for your pond. Among these are zoning laws and fence codes, electric and water supply, hours of direct sun per day, viewing and grading.

A Safe and Legal Pond

ZONING LAWS AND FENCE CODES

You should check with your local borough, township or county zoning office to find

*The ideal setting
for your pond
may be near your
deck.*

out whether there are any special ordinances that would prohibit or restrict the location, size and/or depth of your pond. Do this before you choose the location and size of your pond. In some areas, ponds of a particular size or depth will need to be fenced in to protect small children from accidentally falling in. Ponds, especially those with splashing fountains and waterfalls, will attract children who would not normally wander onto your property. Remember, even a bucket of water can be dangerous to a toddler. In most areas, ponds that are less than 18 inches in depth require no special permits or fencing. If the zoning regulations in your community require your pond to be fenced in, also verify the required height of the fence. Note that many communities have a height limitation for fences reflecting the belief that fences higher that 6 feet tall are an eyesore. In sum, careful compliance with your town's zoning and fencing codes will help to create a safe pond for your enjoyment and will help to mitigate your liability should an accident occur.

CONSULT YOUR INSURANCE AGENT

Ask your agent if your homeowner's insurance covers liability for injuries incurred in connection with a pond or pool. If it does not, your agent may recommend that you update your policy. Doing so will be especially important if you have small children in your neighborhood.

Viewing

If you are going to install a pond, it is, no doubt, because you want to "see" and enjoy it from as many angles
as possible. For example, if you spend many hours
lounging on your deck, perhaps the ideal setting for
your pond is close to your deck. If you also want to be
able to view it from inside your home, a setting that can
be seen from a favorite window might be appropriate.
If you have a large yard, you may choose to create an
"escape" and install your pond farther away from your
house and surround it with benches, swings or other
"people perches."

Sunlight

You will want to choose a site that will receive a minimum of six hours of direct sunlight a day if you plan
to grow Water Lilies and other flowering aquatic
plants. Most Water Lily and Lotus species and cultivars bloom best when they receive between ten and

*Water Lilies need
ten to twelve hours
of sunlight every
day.*

twelve hours of direct sunlight each day. There are
exceptions, however. Sev-
eral cultivars have been
hybridized to require as
few as three hours of sunlight a day. If you plan to
install your pond within
a shade garden, you will
probably not be able to
grow many flowering aqua-
tics, although ponds in
the shade are also lovely.
Ferns, mosses and shade-loving grasses are ideal
choices for this type of pond. Goldfish are also quite
happy in a shade garden.

Trees, Leaves and Falling
Debris

If you've always dreamed of having a pond under the
big oak tree, you should reconsider this location.

Leaves (and other debris) can be deadly to fish and can clog your pump and filtration system. As they decay in the pond, leaves can deplete the pond of oxygen and can make the water dangerously acidic. Installing your pond under deciduous trees will also require much more maintenance to ensure the safety of your fish and the general quality of your water. In addition, the roots of larger trees may eventually penetrate the pond liner, requiring extensive repair work. Note that evergreens are also a danger to successful pondkeeping. Pine trees can be exceptionally harmful if their needles fall into the pond. Do not locate a pond too near to them or plant pine trees near the pond site.

Electric Supply

If your pond will require a pump, filter and/or lighting, you will need to have access to electricity. Household extension cords should not be used. Use only exterior grade, heavy-duty cables (having protective conduit) with three-prong grounded safety plugs. Electrical outlets should be protected with weatherproof covers and cord locks to prevent possible disconnection. All circuitry should be protected by a ground fault circuit interrupter or a residual current circuit breaker with a 30 mA, 30 millisecond rating. If your site is not next to your home, you will have to decide how you will run a line to your pond. Often times this is done by burying an outdoor electric cable underground. This is not a task for the inexperienced, and should be done by a certified electrician.

Water Supply

Of course, you will need to have access to water for filling, cleaning and replacing water due to normal evaporation. If you plan to dig a natural (also called a "clay" or an "earth") bottom pond because you have access to a spring, you should be prepared for the disadvantages of this arrangement. First, you must accept that your pond will probably never be crystal clear. In most instances you will be able to see the fish as they surface to feed, but you will not be able to see down to the bottom of the pond. Spring-fed ponds also require more maintenance to keep native aquatic plants and weeds from germinating and taking over the pond. Some plants, once established, will spread vigorously. Cattails, Rushes, Sedges and a variety of aquatic weeds are fast growers and will need to be kept in check.

Lastly, due to the coldness of the water in a spring-fed pond, some plants may not flourish at all in this environment. Many aquatic plants (particularly hardy Water Lilies and Lotus) need the water temperature maintained at 60°F or higher to bloom. Tropical Water Lilies require an even warmer temperature. Most tropical aquatic plants, such as Taro, tropical Water Lilies and the Cyperus species (Egyptian Paper Plant, Umbrella Palm and Dwarf Papyrus), will surely have a difficult time in a spring-fed pond.

Water test kits are readily available and easy to use.

If you will be using tap water or well water, you will need to be aware of the quality of the water. Well water can be very "hard," and iron and/or other minerals, if present in high levels, may be dangerous to fish and aquatic plants. Iron, in particular, may cause a rusty color to form on plant pots, liners, submersible pumps and filter boxes.

If you are using tap water, check to see if it has been treated using chlorine or chloramines. Chlorine, a

Welcome to
the World of
Pondkeeping

volatile gas, dissipates within forty-eight hours, but chloramines (formed by adding ammonia to chlorine) do not, and the water will have to be treated to remove it. Most treatments available today do not effectively eliminate chloramines completely, so it is best to check the water source first before it is used in your pond. A call to your water company will verify the treatment process used.

> **KEEP WATER SOFTENERS AWAY FROM YOUR POND**
>
> If you have a water softener added to your home water source, you will want to bypass it when filling and topping-up the level of your pond. Water softener systems use solar salts to soften water, which can in turn raise the water's alkalinity. Water that is too alkaline is dangerous to both plants and fish.

Inexpensive, easy-to-use water test kits are available at most garden centers dealing in pond supplies, pond supply shops or pet stores. These kits will help you to determine the levels of a number of elements present in the water, including total hardness, carbonate hardness, pH value, ammonia content and nitrites. Additional information on water quaity will be discussed in Part Three, "Care and Maintenance of Your Garden Pond."

Grading

The grade or slope of the land on which you will install your pond is critically important. Because your pond must be level, you will have to make provisions when excavating your site. Be sure to take precautions to avoid the possibility of water runoff into your pond. If the site has poor drainage, or if you have any underground springs on the site, it may be necessary to install drainage pipes or a stone-filled trench to "absorb" any runoff water that may otherwise flow into your pond. If you have a sloping grade and feel it would be too much trouble, don't give up on your dream. Some of the most beautiful water gardens are built on a slope. You can use the sloping grade to incorporate a wonderful waterfall!

18

chapter 3

Installing
Your Pond

The installation process is, no doubt, the most labor-intensive part of having a pond. Depending upon the size and depth of your pond and the additional design features that you wish to incorporate, such as waterfalls or streams, it can take anywhere from a day to several weeks to install. Smaller ponds can be dug manually using hand tools, such as shovels, picks and spades, but for larger ponds, you will probably have to hire a backhoe operator. You must determine the size and depth that your pond will be before you start to dig.

Pond Depth

Regarding depth, it is widely recommended that the depth of the pond be at least 18 inches. If you live where your growing zone is 4 or below, 24 inches should be the minimum pond depth. The harsh winters and cold temperatures common in the colder climates will cause the pond to freeze down to several inches in depth for long periods of time, thereby requiring a sufficient minimum depth. Moreover, Water Lilies and some other aquatic plants need this depth to develop and flower properly.

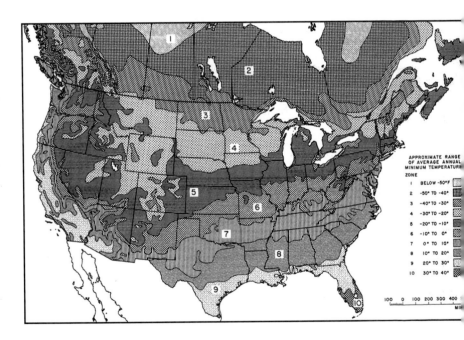

APPROXIMATE RANGE OF AVERAGE ANNUAL MINIMUM TEMPERATURE	
ZONE	
1	BELOW -50°F
2	-50° TO -40°
3	-40° TO -30°
4	-30° TO -20°
5	-20° TO -10°
6	-10° TO 0°
7	0° TO 10°
8	10° TO 20°
9	20° TO 30°
10	30° TO 40°

Your growing zone will have an impact on your pond depth and on the plants that you select for your pond.

Also, if you plan to keep Koi (a colorful Carp that will be discussed later in this book), you will need to provide even greater depth, as Koi can grow as long as 2 feet. To exercise their large muscles, Koi need water that is both deep and wide. A minimum depth of 3 feet is recommended for Koi, although many Koi enthusiasts suggest depths of 5 feet or greater. (Koi are sometimes referred to as common Carp in fancy pajamas!)

Coping and Plant "Shelves"

You will want to consider a planting shelf in your pond installation. Shelves provide a shallow area for marginal plants to be placed. These shelves should be approximately 8 inches deep and 8 to 12 inches wide, and should follow the perimeter of the pond. If you do not include a shelving edge in your pond, you will find yourself looking for ways to keep your marginal plants out of deep water. Unsightly concrete blocks are heavy and undesirable for this use. It's better to make provisions for your marginal plants during the construction phase of your pond than to try to compensate later.

You will also want to provide a shelf for the coping material, such as rock or brick, to set in. You can create a bog area within this level as well by gradually extending the liner out in a gently sloping pattern. Bog plantings are different than marginals as bog plants only require that their "feet" be kept damp, but not necessarily sopping wet.

The effect of these shelves is somewhat like a series of steps, with one being used for the marginal plants and one for the coping material.

Choosing the Liner

There are many kinds of liner available today: concrete, fiberglass, polyethylene, rubber and polyvinyl chloride (PVC). These are described in detail below.

CONCRETE

Concrete, of course, has been in use for decades. However, concrete is difficult to work with, especially for the amateur. Because of the rigid, nonflexible makeup of concrete, ongoing maintenance may be required—particularly in the colder climates where ground and air temperature fluctuation and ground shifting can cause concrete to crack and/or crumble. Additionally, concrete needs to be adequately "leached" before fish and plants can be introduced. This leaching process may take some time before all the lime in the concrete has been removed. Sealers can be (and should be) used on concrete ponds.

FIBERGLASS LINERS

Molded fiberglass liners have also been used in the past, but they are extremely expensive, heavy and difficult to ship and to install. Although this type of preformed liner is still available, it is not widely used by hobbyists.

POLYETHYLENE LINERS

Use of the fiberglass preformed liners has declined, and the current preference is for the newer polyethylene liners (sometimes referred to as "rigid" liners). These liners (usually black in color) are lightweight but heavy-duty, designed to withstand the hottest summers and the harshest winters. They come in a variety of sizes and shapes. Polyethylene cascading waterfalls are also available to complement the preformed ponds. However, depending upon the manufacturer, the rim of the preformed ponds may be difficult to hide. Some of the rims or lips are rolled or have a bulky edge that can be awkward to work with. Usually, flat stones are used as coping and laid on top of the rim around the edge of the pond. When excavating the site where the preformed pond will go, it is important to dig the hole so that the liner fits the hole quite snugly. Try to avoid having to backfill because the hole was dug too large, as this could cause the pond to shift and tiny sinkholes to form where the backfill was placed. You will also want to place a few inches of sand on the bottom of the excavated hole to cushion the pond. Preformed ponds are great starter ponds for entry-level pondkeepers. They are small enough to maintain yet large enough to give the new hobbyist adequate space in which to experiment and learn the basics of pondkeeping.

RUBBER LINERS

Flexible and durable, these are the liners of choice for most pondkeepers today. The rubber sheets are constructed of a synthetic polymer called EPDM (ethylene/propylene/diene/monmer) and are most often available in a thickness of approximately 45 mil. This material resembles EPDM roofing liner but is manufactured specifically for pond use. When purchasing an EPDM liner, be sure the words "fish friendly" appear on the liner and/or on the packaging. Many people have reported using the roof-grade rubber with no ill effects, but the manufacturers do not recommend this as it is possible for harmful chemicals to leach from the roof-grade liner material, causing toxic conditions for fish and plants.

Rubber liners are very flexible, allowing the installer to mold them around curves and corners. They are not susceptible to ultraviolet (UV) damage by the sun and are difficult to puncture. If a puncture should occur, repair kits are readily available and relatively inexpensive. Rubber liners also have a long life. Most manufacturers guarantee them for twenty or more years, but the life expectancy is projected at more than forty years. PondGard™, manufactured by Firestone Building Products, is the trade name of the most widely available brand.

Rubber liners are flexible and easily molded.

When using a rubber liner, it is recommended that a 1- to 2-inch layer of sand be placed in the bottom of the pond to protect the liner from possible punctures from rock or stone. In extremely rocky conditions, it is suggested that a underlay be used. This strong fiber provides extra protection from sharp rocks and other objects that may work their way to the surface. Some people use layers of newspapers (1 to 1½ inches) or carpet remnants to accomplish this goal and have reported good results. This liner is usually black in color and can be purchased on rolls or folded. It is often sold in combination with a pump and filter box as a "package deal" by some distributors.

23

Butyl is another type of rubber liner more commonly used in the U.K., but available in the U.S. as well. It is a heavier rubber (about 60 mil.) than the synthetic polymer liners and is a little more difficult to work with. It is also much more expensive than EPDM. Manufacturers claim that it will last fifty or more years.

PVC LINERS

Until recently, polyvinyl chloride (PVC) was also used as liner material for ponds. However, PVC, a plastic material, did not have a long life and was very susceptible to UV rays, which break down and weaken the material. PVC is not flexible like EPDM and efforts to stretch it to conform to angles and corners can lead to weak spots, rips and punctures. It has an estimated life span of only four to five years and needs to be replaced much more often than a rubber liner. It also does not hold up well in the colder climates. PVC, or even plastic sheeting material, might serve the purpose quite well for an indoor pool, where temperature changes and ultraviolet rays are minimal.

Calculating the Size of Liner Needed

For a first-time pond installer, it is easy to misunderstand the amount of liner you will need. Some "pond-in-a-box" kits will state that the kit includes an 8 by 10 foot liner, but this does not mean that you will get an 8 by 10 foot pond! If you dig an 8 by 10 foot hole with a maximum depth of 2 feet, you will need a liner that is 14 feet by 16 feet. To obtain the proper measurement for the liner, multiply the desired pond width by twice the maximum pond depth, and then add 2 feet (1 foot for each edge). Make the same calculation for the desired length of the pond. Liners are available in almost any size. You will also need to add separate liner pieces for streams, waterfalls or any other element that will need to contain water. These can be seamed to your main liner. As with the pond liner, the liner for other elements will have to accommodate the depth of the element.

Excavation

Once you have decided on the liner you will use for your pond, it will be time to excavate the soil. If you are fortunate enough to have good soil to work with, the job will be a lot less laborious, but time and care must still be taken. If your soil is extremely rocky or is comprised of heavy clay, you may need to have it excavated using a backhoe rather than by hand shovel.

BASIC TOOLS

You will need several basic tools to assist you in the excavation process: a long rope(s) or garden hose to lay out the size and shape of your pond on the site itself and a can of white or brightly colored spray paint (I prefer neon pink!) to mark the outline. Be sure to have various types and sizes of shovels, spades and pick axes on hand to loosen and remove the soil. You will need a spirit level and a straightedge (such as a 2 inch by 4 inch by 8 foot board) or stakes and string. You will also need a wheelbarrow for transporting the soil away from the site or for moving it to the side of the pond in which you will install the waterfall. If your pond is to be larger than 15 feet in diameter, you may want to find someone who has access to (and can use) a transit. A transit is a surveying instrument that measures angles.

The water in the pond acts as a level on its own! It will not matter if the bottom of the pond is sloping or flat, the water will always be level in the pond. It is the ground around the perimeter of the pond that will need to be leveled. This should be done before the actual excavation takes place.

START DIGGING

Once you have your tools gathered, you can proceed with the actual excavation. First, using the garden hose or rope, lay out the shape and size of the pond, taking care not to create drastic back curves or angles. You will want the water to circulate in the pond without creating "pockets" into which water and debris may become trapped and unable to move freely. Algae, the pond's biggest nemesis, are also more likely to form in these areas.

Using the spray paint, make a line just outside the hose or rope layout. If you are installing a rigid preformed pond, you can use the liner itself as your layout. Be sure not to get paint on the liner. Some people use chalk or flour instead of paint to mark their guide. (This works best on smaller ponds that can be dug in a few hours.) Be sure you make the paint line heavy enough to see clearly and so that it will last for the duration of the excavation. This painted line will serve as your guide throughout the excavation process.

Next, using a spade or shovel, begin to dig from just inside the outline, making sure to dig vertically, as ponds (with the exception of larger ponds with gradually sloping sides) should have vertical sides. Vertical sides help to hide the liner and to deter algae growth. You will dig the coping shelf first, followed by the plant shelf, then the interior of the pond. As mentioned previously, the effect should be step-like in appearance.

Be sure to dig your pond so that it will have vertical sides.

Once the soil has been excavated from the pond, you can use it to build up the grade for a waterfall at one end. Be sure that all visible rocks and other objects are removed from the pond before you add the sand or other underlay material. If you notice any tree roots coming from the sides, you could be in for trouble. Make sure you are not installing your pond under or too close to a tree. Roots of most mature trees do not grow any wider than the widest branch, so you can use this as a gauge as to how large the root system is (or will be) underground. For many reasons, it is not a good idea to site your pond too near to or under a tree.

DRAINAGE AND OVERFLOW PROVISIONS

3

For small ponds (under 5,000 gallons), it is not necessary to provide a bottom drain or an overflow pipe. It is quite easy to keep the water level in check in a small pond unless torrential rains cause the water to run over the edge. If this should happen, you can simply bail some of the water out of the pond or siphon the water with a hose to help direct the water away from the edge of the pond. Or, during the construction process, you may make one small section of the edge a bit lower and create a stone or pea gravel trench lead-

By sloping the ground away from the pond, you will help direct water away from the edge.

ing from this low area so that the water will be directed to the lower end and through the trench during rainy periods. If the water spills over the edge for a duration of time, water may get behind the liner and cause problems, particularly in rubber and flexible liner ponds where the water may cause the liner to lift. If you slope the ground away from the pond during the excavation process, this will also help direct water away from the pond's edge.

For larger ponds, you should install a bottom drain. This will involve more complicated excavation and plumbing. Unless you know how to do plumbing work, it's probably a good idea to have someone else construct your pond for you or at least oversee the plumbing installation.

A large pond should also have an overflow pipe installed. As water rises during periods of rain, the overflow pipe channels the water out and away from the pond to avoid flooding and/or water under the liner. As with the bottom drain, an overflow pipe requires plumbing work to be done during the excavation process.

After you have completely excavated the dirt, rock and rubble from the pond site, lay the sand or underlay material. If the soil is rocky, underlay should be placed around the sides of the pond as well as the bottom to protect the liner from any protruding rocks or rock fragments that can poke a hole through it over time.

Once the underlay is in place, the liner can now be installed. Unfold or unroll the liner until it is flat. Starting at opposite ends, bring both sides together until the ends meet in the middle and lay them down to cause a fold. Then, depending upon the size, do this again. Repeat with the other two sides. Bring this small, folded liner "packet" and place it in the middle of the pond bottom. Then unfold it out and toward the edges. This simplifies the liner installation process and helps you to evenly distribute the liner. Working from the center of the pond, smooth the liner into place,

If you want a waterfall in your pond, include it during the construction process.

working it into the corners and conforming it to the sides. Use several bricks or rocks to hold the liner down to the ground at the edge.

ADDING A WATERFALL

If a waterfall is to be a part of your pond, this will be the time to construct it. Working with the tamped mound of soil you placed at the waterfall site, excavate a small pool at the top of the falls that leads to cascading steps down toward the pond as desired. Be sure it is deep enough so that when you lay the liner and add the stone, water will not flow over the sides of the waterfall. At the bottom of the waterfall, you will need to seam the two liners together. (Detailed instructions are included with EPDM seaming kits.) Lay flat stones at the base of each tier of the cascade to create a weir for the water to pass over. Smaller, rounder rocks can be placed along the sides to hide the liner and give a more natural look to the falls. If you will be adding a waterfall, you will need a pump to keep the water recirculating. At this time, you will have to decide how you will hide the tubing that will carry the water to the top of the falls.

Now, you can slowly begin to fill the pond using a garden hose. This is an exciting time during the pond-building experience—the turning point, where your hard work starts to become gratifying! As the pond fills you can start to imagine brightly colored Water Lilies floating on the surface as Goldfish nibble at the lily pads looking for a tasty tidbit. As the water fills, continue to smooth and flatten the liner against the earth to limit the number of creases in the liner. Turn the water off when you have filled the pond up to the coping shelf.

Choices of Coping Material

How you finish the edge of your pond is a very individual decision. Rocks and fieldstone are used most of the time because they are inexpensive and easy to find. "Rock hunting" has become somewhat of a hobby for me and my family. Interesting finds include various fossil rocks that we have used as "specimen pieces" around our pond.

Sandstone, slate and granite are all good coping choices. Although beautiful, limestone should be avoided if it will come in contact with the water. It can cause lime to be leached into the pond, raising the pH level, sometimes to danger-

> **AVOID CHEMICALLY TREATED WOOD**
>
> Chemically treated wood should not be used inside the pond, but may be used around the edge (so long as the water does not touch it). If you wish to use wood (for example, vertical timbers tied together to give a pier-like look), select pressure-treated (nonchemically treated) wood. Pressure-treated hardwood has a long life expectancy in the water and weathers and ages beautifully.

ous and, in extreme cases, lethal levels. Whatever your choice, be sure that the stone, brick or other coping choice is not toxic.

INSTALLING THE COPING

Place the coping material on the coping shelf so that it hangs over the shelf edge by about 1 or 2 inches. This will help hide the liner under the shelf and will create a more natural looking transition to the plant shelf below. Make sure that the stones lie flat and are not wobbly when set in place. By stacking several layers of stones, you can enhance the natural appearance of the pond while creating a nice transition from water to land. Stones with flat bottoms and tops are good choices for the coping. Continue the coping around the perimeter of the pond. The top stone, called the "capstone," should extend over the ground by a few inches, giving stability to the edge of the pond and hiding the ends of the liner. Always be mindful of safety. If someone happens to stand on the coping (you'll find people doing this to get even closer to see the fish), you will not want them to lose their footing and possibly fall as a result of a loose or wobbly capstone.

The Mechanics: Pumps, Filters and Skimmers

Congratulations! The most time-consuming and difficult part of building a garden pond is over and you can now move on to the more enjoyable aspects of pondkeeping! In this section, I will discuss the use of pumps, skimmers and various filtration methods available to help keep your pond water clean, clear and healthy.

Layers of flat stones provide a handsome transition from water to land.

Although a pond can survive without them (by using "natural" or alternative methods), most people opt to add a pump and filter system to their pond. Pumps help to aerate the pond (to add oxygen to the water by forcing air through the water), which in turn helps to keep your plants and fish happier and healthier. Pumps are also a crucial part of the filtration process, as pumps pull debris into the filter chamber where the particles are trapped and, depending on the type of filter media used, harmful organic wastes are broken down by bacteria. Pumps move the water through waterfalls or fountains, which results in aeration and circulation. This circulation also adds movement and incredibly soothing sounds to your garden. An unfiltered pond must have the ideal conditions to remain healthy and clear. It is not easy to achieve these conditions in smaller ponds, so it is advisable to use some type of pump and filter system.

Choosing the Right Pump

Pumps for small ponds are submersible, which means that they are placed under the water in the pond itself. They are very easy to install, providing you follow the manufacturer's instructions. You do not have to be a "mechanically inclined" person to learn how to install a pump and understand how it works. There are many varieties and sizes of pumps on the market. You may become confused as to which pump will be the best for you and your pond. All pumps come with certain information printed right on the box, which will help you to decipher which would be best for your particular situation. This information includes the GPH (gallons per hour), the energy efficiency (the maximum power consumption), the type of motor, whether it is oil- or water-cooled and the flow rate. Most pumps also come with a warranty varying from one year to three years. Some pumps are packaged as kits, containing an attachable filter box or basket, an adjustable waterfall tee and fountain head(s). Pumps also come with a variety of cord lengths—some as long as 20 feet—so you'll want to be sure you take that into consideration when choosing your pump. All pumps are black in color so that they are nearly invisible in the pond. When placing your submersible pump in the pond, it is advisable to place it on top of a brick or two. This will help keep the working parts of the pump from getting clogged with debris that settles to the bottom of the pond.

Oil-Cooled vs. Water-Cooled Pumps

I would recommend choosing a pump that has a water-cooled motor rather than one that utilizes an oil-cooled motor. If the seal to the motor compartment (which encases the oil) should leak or completely fall apart while in the water, you will have a messy oil slick in your pond, which is both difficult to remove and dangerous to all pond life. I have talked to many pond owners who have experienced a blown seal on an oil-cooled pump, and believe me, you don't want your pond to be added to the casualty list! The oil sticks to all solid objects in the pond, including plants, plant pots, pond sides, filter boxes and pond critters. Consumer reports indicate that oil-cooled pumps seem to be prone to this problem after the second season. Once a seal on a pump has blown or begun to leak, it cannot be fixed. You certainly will not have this problem with water-cooled pumps.

The size of the pump should depend on the water volume in your pond and the flow rate desired for either (or both) waterfall or fountain. The pump should be able to "turn the water over" at least once every three hours. That is, if your pond holds 1,000 gallons of water, the pump should turn over approximately 333 gallons per hour. For this particular pond, you'll need a pump that has a rated GPH at over 333.

As the pump pushes water through the hose and up the grade to the top of the waterfall, it slowly loses pressure, decreasing flow rate. There is not much of a problem when the grade is slight, but there might be a huge pres-sure loss at 10 feet or greater. Most pumps have a rated GPH at 5 feet. You will want to buy a larger pump if the water will be pumped at lengths longer than 5 feet.

FILTER PADS, BOXES AND BASKETS

Almost all pumps, even the "minipumps," come equipped with some type of filter pad, box or basket. These tiny pumps have a mesh-type filter pad in the pump housing to protect the impeller (the fanlike rotor that pulls the water into the pump) from becoming entangled with debris that can choke the motor, causing it to stop, overheat and burn out. Many of the larger submersible pumps come with a detachable filter box or basket. Water and debris are pulled by the pump through these filters. About once every week or two it is necessary to detach the filter box and clean it to remove the debris. This takes just a few minutes and is done by simply hosing it off with plain water. If algae begins to grow on the pump, hose or filter box, use a soft brush to loosen it while hosing it off with plain water. Never use detergents or bleaches on your pump or filter equipment. The residue can be harmful to the water quality. Weekly or biweekly maintenance keeps the pump working efficiently and keeps the water quality healthy. If you notice that your filter needs to be cleaned more often than once a week, it is probably too small for your pond, and a larger filter should be considered. All pumps and filter boxes come with easy-to-understand instructions.

MAKING YOUR OWN FILTER BOX

If your pump did not come with a filter box, it is relatively easy to make your own. Using a black, plastic aquatic plant pot that is large enough to contain your pump, place the pump into the pot and cover it with a piece of filter pad or fiberglass window screen. Slowly lower the pot into the bottom of the pond. It may be necessary to weight the pot/pump ensemble. You can do this by putting a layer of river rock or pea gravel on the bottom of the pot. As well as weighting your pot, the gravel will act as a small biological filter. Bacteria colonizing on the gravel will help in the filtration process! You can also use this method on a larger pump, but the pot filter would act as a pre-filter box, which would pump the water through a biological filter located outside the pond, then back into the pond. This gives you the advantage of protecting your submersible pump from larger debris that can clog the impeller, while filtering your water via biofiltration.

Welcome to
the World of
Pondkeeping

*Almost all pumps
come equipped
with a filter.*

THE IMPORTANCE OF FILTRATION

Larger ponds require larger filtration systems to keep the water quality clean and clear. There are many fine filtration systems on the market, or you can make your own. The topic of filtration is quite fascinating and can be simple or quite complex. Entire books and videos have been devoted to the subject of filtration. There is really just one reason why the pond hobbyist wants and needs filtration, and

that is to keep the water in his or her pond clean and clear so that the fish and plants can be seen and enjoyed. Filtration, in simple terms, moves the pond water through a container of filtration media. There are two basic types of filtration methods: mechanical and biological. Often you will find a combination of these two methods used in the same filter system. This type of combination filter is what I prefer to use.

A mechanical filter uses traps and contains debris and larger particles that are then removed by the pond-keeper on a weekly or biweekly maintenance schedule. This debris may include leaves, uneaten fish food, mulch or other ground particles (which have been accidentally kicked into the pond), dead aquatic plant debris, algae particles and so on.

Biological filtration (conducted by "biofilters") depends on a colony of beneficial bacteria called nitrosonomas and nitrobacter (which are alive and growing naturally in most ponds) to purify the water. As the pond water moves over and through the filter media, the bacteria "eat" the dissolved organic wastes, converting harmful ammonia into nitrite and then into harmless nitrate. Biofilters do not remove algae nor do they remove large particles. This is why a combination of both mechanical and biological filtration methods is best.

An operational biofilter does not need to be cleaned more often than once or twice a year. If you clean it, it actually removes the bacteria that are essential to the effectiveness of the biofilter. Since it relies on "live" organisms, a biofilter will not work properly when the temperatures drop below 55°F. Also, once a biofilter system is established, it should not be turned off (except for winter months), as this will cause the bac-teria to be

Water will con-stantly move over this biofilter in-stalled beneath a future waterfall.

teria to die. Keep the pump operating twenty-four hours per day. A variety of media can be used to "grow" these biological beds, and the choice is up to the individual pondkeeper. The most popular choices include river rock (1 to 1½ inches in diameter), lava rock, pea gravel and lightweight plastic objects such as hair rollers. Manufac-turers have devised other media such as plastic balls called "bio-balls," which look like tiny Wiffle™ balls. These, however, can be expensive, and hobbyists have found that simple, inex-pensive media, such as river rock, is the more practical choice.

If a biological filter system seems to be overloaded or not working properly, chances are the pond has been stocked with too many fish. A heavy fish load creates an excessive amount of waste material, which bogs down the filter system, causing it to be ineffective.

Skimmers

Skimmers are most often used on ponds that are larger than 6 feet in diameter. A skimmer can consist of a "multiple method" filtration system incorporating skimming, mechanical and biofiltration into one unit. The skimmer is located on the outside of the pond but installed into the ground on the same level as the pond. Skimmers look like large garbage cans and can be square or round in shape. The pump is placed in the bottom of the skimmer rather than in the pond itself. The pump pulls the water and surface debris through an opening in the side of the skimmer where the debris is deposited into a catch net. The water, finer particles and dissolved organic matter continue through filter pads that trap the larger particles before they get pushed back out through the pump, through a hose and on their way to the waterfalls or fountainhead. Several inches of biofiltration material (river stone, lava rock and the like) are located in the bottom of the skimmer, which forms a perfect place for bacteria to colonize.

Additional care must be taken to be sure the skimmer does not become clogged with too much debris. If this should happen, water will not be able to move freely into the skimmer chamber, the pump will become dry and the motor will overheat and burn out. Although they require a more intensive installation, skimmer systems are well worth the price and time spent in their assemblage.

Whatever pump and filtration method(s) you choose, be sure to select the right equipment for the job. For peak performance, keep the equipment clean and in good condition.

Ultraviolet Sterilizers

Ultraviolet (UV) sterilizers are used primarily to kill algae spores that cause green water. UV sterilizers work by destroying the DNA within the algae cells. The algae cells must be exposed to the UV rays (generated by the lamp) for sufficient time and at a high enough wattage. Various manufacturers recommend different flow rates and wattages. Some contend that because the cells pass through the UV system repeatedly, less wattage is needed, while others take a more conservative view and recommend higher wattage and lower

> ### CONSIDER UNDERWATER LIGHTS
>
> Underwater lights can illuminate the entire interior of the pond to enable you to see the fish and aquatic plants long after the sun goes down. Colored filters are also available, allowing you to cast a blue, red, green, gold or even a purple tint into the water. Underwater lights don't really look natural, but if placed correctly, they can be stunning additions to your pond.

flow rates. One thing to remember when choosing a UV sterilizer is that the strength of a UV emitter lessens over time, and even though the light bulb is lit, it may not be emitting enough UV rays for your particular application.

UV sterilizers are expensive, but they are an almost certain cure for green water, no matter what the temperature, pH or other environmental factors. UV sterilizers also help to reduce disease pathogens and dramatically reduce filter clogging because there are no algae cells to clog the filter media.

As a rule, pondkeepers should try the natural approach before adding a UV sterilizer to their pond.

Lighting Your Garden Pond

Ponds can be enjoyed not only during the daylight hours, but also well into evening. By lighting the exterior of your pond with low-voltage lights, you can create an inexpensive nighttime retreat for your family and friends.

Underwater lights are stunning additions to a pond.

Outdoor lighting products come in a variety of styles, ranging from the common plastic pathway stake lights to those done in brass in the forms of mushrooms, Trumpet Lilies and other garden objects. Exterior lights should be positioned to light pathways (if you would like to stroll around your pond in the evening) or to showcase the waterfalls, a fountain or your favorite specimen plants.

There are also underwater lighting kits available to light up the interior of the pond or under the waterfalls. Floodlights can illuminate the entire pond and garden area at night; however, the effects are not as dramatic as with carefully positioned spot lighting.

Stocking

part two

Your
Pond

chapter 4

Aquatic
Plants

Now that the construction of your pond has been completed and the pump and filtration system are in operation, it's time for your pond to come to life! I look at a newly constructed pond as a "canvas" ready for wonderful textures and colors to be added that will slowly turn your pond into a work of art! Stocking the pond with plants, fish, tadpoles, snails and other critters is wonderful fun, and caring for them can be a year-round hobby for the entire family. Children love to watch fish swim and eat, and they'll spend hours looking for frogs and snails at the water's edge. If you have children, encourage their interest. Taking care of a pond is a wonderful way to help children learn about caring for the environment!

Stocking your garden pond provides you with endless choices. The word to remember is "balance." With all the beautiful plants and fish to choose from, it is easy to overstock the pond with too much of a good thing. A good rule of thumb for stocking a new pond is that you should have no more than 1 inch of fish per square foot of surface water. Exceeding this rule will create a heavy fish load, resulting in too much fish waste for the filter to adequately address. Once a pond has been established, the load can be increased to about 2 inches per square foot. Remember that the little 2-inch Goldfish will quickly become a 6-inch adult—but the fish-to-water formula will not change. Do not overstock your new pond with too many fish!

The same principle applies to plants—don't over-crowd. You want to be able to see the water and the fish in it! Use enough marginals to soften the edge and enough floating foliage plants to cover about sixty to seventy percent of the pond's surface. Submerged plants should be stocked at one established plant per every 2 square feet of space.

The Abundance of Plants

Most people are surprised to learn just how many aquatic plant species and cultivars there are to be enjoyed in the garden pond. There are so many, in fact, that there is no reason why something can't be blooming in your pond from early spring through the end of fall. Growing aquatic plants is probably the easiest form of gardening. Aquatic plants require very little mainte-nance and, with a few exceptions, they are resistant to most pests. Aquatic plants are generally broken down into two groups: hardy plants and tropical plants. In the colder growing zones, the hardy plants may be treated as though they were perennials, (having a life cycle of more than two years) and tropicals may be treated as though they were annuals. In growing zone 10, south-ern Florida, and zone 11, south of the mainland (see chapter 3), most tropicals will thrive without any special care during the winter months, although a hard frost could be devastating to them.

In addition to their beauty, aquatic plants are very beneficial to the health of the pond. They absorb nutrients
that would otherwise feed algae. They provide forag-
ing areas for fish and other pond life as well as giving them a place to mate and lay their eggs. Finally,
plants give the baby fish a place to hide from hungry
predators.

*Aquatic plants
absorb nutrients
that would other-
wise feed algae.*

Algae

Algae are aquatic plants in their simplest form. A mem-
ber of the plant group, thallophytes, algae are said to
be the nemesis of the pond, but they are also a necessary component of a balanced ecosystem. There are
over 17,000 varieties of algae, so you are bound to get
a few varieties in your pond!

Algae are the most important food producers in the
aquatic environment. Filaments of algae that form
the familiar stringy looking "pond scum" harbor many
microscopic animals, called plankton or zooplankton.
Without this food source, much of the other pond
life will not be able to exist. A pond without algae in
it is simply not a healthy pond. Almost without exception, a new pond will experience an initial "algae
bloom" period that could last for several weeks. The
water will look cloudy, sometimes brown or green
in color. This is caused by single-celled algae that, like
all algae, contain chlorophyll and often other pigments. Sometimes these single-celled algae will join

together to form chainlike filaments; others "swim" like single-celled animals. If the pond has the right balance of fish and plants, and the water depth is 18 inches or greater, this bloom should slowly subside, and clear water will prevail!

In manufacturing food, algae release oxygen, which increases the amount of oxygen that is dissolved in the pond water. When there are too many algae, however, they may deplete the pond of oxygen levels as they die and decay. This could be the reason for a midsummer algae bloom.

There are countless incidents where entry-level pond-keepers become so frustrated with algae growth that they constantly empty their ponds, scrub the liner and refill with new water in an attempt to rid their pond of it. This starts them off at "ground zero" again, creating a perfect condition (tap water is full of nutrients) for yet another algae bloom. If they continue this practice, their ponds will never become established. So, please, let the initial algae bloom be!

By following a few simple rules, you should be able to keep your pond from becoming overrun by algae. These rules include:

1. Do not stock your pond with too many fish, because algae thrive on fish waste.

2. Be sure you stock your pond with enough plant material to effectively compete for nutrients that algae need. Be sure the water surface is at least sixty percent covered by floating aquatic plants and Water Lily pads. These help shield the water from excessive sunlight, which promotes algae growth.

With sufficient water depth and the right mix of fish and plants, clear water will prevail!

3. Be sure your pump and filtration system are operating effectively and are kept clean.

4. Hairlike "blue-green string" algae (sometimes referred to as blanket weed) and the "bubbling" green algae should be pulled from the pond whenever possible. You can do this by hand or by twisting it on a stick. Plastic spaghetti forks work very well for this purpose! Discard the algae in a compost bin or throw it away. If you seem to have a lot of the bubbling green algae, it is a sign that there is decaying matter in the pond—usually decaying leaves from trees or dead aquatic plants.

Floating Plants

Floating plants such as Water Hyacinths, Duckweed and Water Lettuce float, unanchored, on the surface of the water with their roots dangling into the water below. These plants get all of their nutrients from the water by root absorption. All floating varieties are tropical plants and will not overwinter well. The root systems on the larger varieties may grow extremely long and may have to be trimmed from time to time throughout the growing season. Floating plants make an excellent place for fish to lay their eggs and for fry to hide from predators. Before separating or trimming the floating plants, check to see if there are eggs on the underside of the plant or entangled in the root system. If so, you may want to wait a few days until the eggs have hatched before removing or trimming the plant(s). Following are some of the many available varieties of aquatic floating plants.

Water Lettuce floats on the surface of the water.

DUCKWEED (*Lemna minor*)

Duckweed is a tiny plant (each leaf is less than ⅛ inch in diameter). It is an excellent natural food for Goldfish and other pond fish. Duckweed is aggressive in its growing habit, and if fish are not present, it can quickly cover the surface of your pond.

FAIRY MOSS (*Azolla caroliniana*)

Fairy Moss is an attractive floating fern. Fairy Moss is seen in both bright green and burgundy colors. The green color darkens to crimson or rust towards fall. The leaves range between $\frac{1}{4}$ and $\frac{1}{2}$ inch in diameter. Koi love to eat and forage through this plant. Be aware, however, that Fairy Moss is a strong survivor and can be invasive if not kept in check.

WATER VELVET (*Salvinia auriculata*)

Water Velvet is a larger floating plant than the Duckweed or Fairy Moss. It is very unusual and has round, hairy, pale-green leaves up to $\frac{3}{4}$ inch long, which are formed in rolling strands.

WATER LETTUCE (*Pistia*)

Water Lettuce is a larger, rosette-shaped plant. It is medium green in color. The underside of the leaf takes on a lighter color and has a feltlike texture. Each rosette sends out "babies" on the end of runners throughout the growing season. One plant can easily fill a pond by the end of the growing season! It is best to monitor the population of Water Lettuce and to keep it in check by discarding older plants or those turning yellow.

The Water Hyacinth's lavender flowers stand well above the foliage.

WATER HYACINTH (*Eichornia crassipes*)

Water Hyacinth is a flowering aquatic plant. The waxy-green foliage is comprised of leaves at the end of air-filled, bulblike stems. The Water Hyacinth is a larger plant, and these bulbs give the plant buoyancy to keep it afloat. The intense lavender-blue flowers stand well above the foliage in clusters, with each flower resembling an orchid. They are beautiful, but can become very invasive. Water Hyacinths are illegal in the state of Florida and in some other areas because of their ability to completely choke out waterways and prohibit passage of boats. However, they usually cannot withstand a killing frost, and are therefore a safe plant choice for most parts of the United States.

Shallow Plants

Bog plants like to "keep their feet wet," but they do not like to be totally immersed in the water. They thrive where their roots can remain moist throughout the growing season.

Marginals are plants that like to have their crown covered by water, but by no more than a few inches. The variety of marginal plants is seemingly endless. There are grasses, such as sedges and rushes, which soften the edge of the pond and create a graceful transition from water to land. Some of the grasses send up inflorescence (clusters of flowerlike seed heads) on stalks. Some varieties can be somewhat showy, but may lack color and brilliance. Selections of aquatic grasses include the following.

There are several varieties of Cattails from which to choose.

Cattail (*Typha*)

There are several varieties of Cattails from which to choose. The inflorescence are quite bold and make a stunning, yet natural-looking backdrop for the garden pond. Among this family, popular varieties are as follows.

Common Cattail (Latifolia)

The Common Cattail is a bold, vertical accent plant that is hardy to zone 3. It has invasive runners that, left uncontained, will completely take over the pond in a few short years. It can grow to over 6 feet and has large, brown Cattail "catkins" in the summer.

Graceful Cattail (*Typha angustifolia*)

This Cattail is similar to the Common Cattail except it has thin, graceful and slender foliage and sprouts small, thin catkins in the summer.

Miniature Cattail (*Typha minima*)

A Miniature Cattail is perfect for the small pond or container pond. It has petite, round catkins and grows to just 18 inches. It is hardy to zone 3.

SWEETFLAG (*Acorus calamus*)

Sweetflags are tall (2 to 3 inches), with swordlike blades. This hardy plant is also available in a variegated form (*Acorus calamus "Variegatus"*), which has green and cream vertical stripes. Sweetflag emits a sweet scent when a leaf is broken.

SPIKE RUSH (*Eleocharis montevidensis*)

The Spike Rush is a small (1 inch) grass that has quill-like spikes from a central clump. It has tiny brown inflorescence

The variegated form of Sweetflag has green and cream stripes.

on each spike when the plant matures. Spike Rush may be grown as a bog or marginal plant and will often grow in marshy areas as well. This plant, with its spiky foliage, resembles a clump of fiber optics!

CHINESE WATER CHESTNUT (*Eleocharis tubersosa*)

The Chinese Water Chestnut has attractive bright green stems that are hollow. They illuminate in the sun adding interest and variety to the edges of the pond. They grow to 2 inches and are hardy to zone 8.

VARIEGATED STRIPED RUSH (*Baumea rubiginosa*)

The Variegated Striped Rush has stiff, green, swordlike foliage with vertical bright yellow stripes. It is semi-evergreen and grows to 2 inches.

*The Common
Yellow Iris pro-
duces masses of
tall blossoms.*

Flowering Marginal Plants

There are flowering marginals, which give bursts of color to the pond's edge for a short period.

IRISES

The aquatic Iris varieties bloom in the spring, usually lasting no more than a week, but their bladelike foliage continues to add height and texture to the edge of the pond throughout the summer and into fall. If you want a jump start on spring color in the garden pond, Iris varieties are the way to go. Make sure your camera is loaded before they begin to bloom, as you will not want to miss out on taking pictures of these truly regal aquatic plant specimens!

Most Irises are hardy to zone 4 and come in a wide variety of colors, including blue, deep purple, lavender, pink, white, rose and yellow. They multiply via their root system, and within just a few years, a single plant can garner several dozen! Here are several favorite Irises to be used as marginals in the garden pond.

Pseudacorus

Pseudacorus is the Common Yellow Iris. It grows to 4 feet in height and is European in its origin. It produces masses of canary yellow blossoms that stand above the tall, erect foliage. The blossoms are not large, but because of the quantity of the blossoms and the brilliant yellow color, they are quite striking.

Versicolor

Versicolor is the most popular and most widely distributed Iris. It is a North American native and can often be seen growing and blooming along ditches, streams and other natural water sources throughout much of the United States. It grows to 2 feet, making it one of the smallest of the Iris varieties. Versicolor boasts beautiful royal blue to violet blossoms and medium green foliage that keeps its color throughout most of the summer. It is a very profuse bloomer, blossoming in the spring.

Laevigata *has beautiful white flowers.*

Laevigata *"Snowdrift"*

Laevigata grows to just 2 feet in height, but has quite a long blooming period in the spring. The graceful white flowers have violet centers or speckles, which add to the beauty. The foliage is a rich, green color.

Louisiana Iris "Black Gamecock"

The Louisiana Iris "Black Gamecock" tends to bloom a little later than the *Pseudacorus* and Versicolor. It grows to 3 feet in height and has large, deep purple to midnight blue (almost black) blossoms that sit atop medium green foliage. They look beautiful when planted in combination with *Laevigata* "Snowdrift."

Louisiana Iris "Kissie"

This Iris has large blossoms that bloom a little later in the spring. The deep pink petals pale or dissolve to a soft yellow in the center of the blossom. The foliage is rich green in color.

Pseudacorus *"Flore Plena"*

Pseudacorus "Flore Plena" is similar to the *Pseudacorus* with the exception that it has "double" blossoms. The massive blossoms are almost "canna-like" in their appearance and attract attention from a distance. This Iris grows to 4 feet tall, towering over some of the other Iris species.

Iris "Rose Queen"

Iris "Rose Queen" is a dainty Iris with soft, lavender pink blossoms. It is a good clumping variety and blooms later in the spring. The foliage is grasslike, which sets off the blooms quite gracefully. It can reach 2 feet in height.

Louisiana Iris "Clyde Redmond"

This Iris variety is one of the most beautiful blue Irises. It grows to 3 feet, having impressive medium green foliage and vibrant, full, royal blue blossoms.

Virginica

Virginica is a North American native that is occasionally confused with Versicolor. It is a larger Iris than Versicolor, growing to 3 feet and having a deeper color, ranging from deep blue to violet. The foliage is also richer and more striking than that of the Versicolor.

Lamance Iris (Brevicaulis)

This Iris is quite small, growing to no more than 18 inches in height. It has delicate blue flowers above broad and weeping foliage. It is the last Iris to bloom during the spring and is a true North American native.

Ensata (Iris kaempferi)

Ensata is a Japanese Iris. It grows to 2 feet and has large purple and/or white blossoms that are held high above rich green foliage. It is a good choice for a specimen plant.

OTHER FLOWERING MARGINALS

Of course, in addition to Iris and the other marginal plants listed previously in this chapter, there are many other flowering marginals to choose from including:

Four-Leaf Water Clover *(Marsilea)*, Water Pennywort *(Hydrocotyle verticillata)*, Marsh Marigold *(Caltha palustris)*, Button Bush *(Cephalanthus occidentalis)*, Hardy Orchid *(Bletilla striata)*, Water Poppy *(Hydrocleys nymphoides)*, Cardinal Flower *(Lobelia cardinalis)*, Loosestrife *(Lythrum salicaria)*, Scarlet Rosemallow *(Hibiscus moschuetos)*, Lizard's Tail *(Saururus cernuus)*, Water Alyssum *(Samolus parviflorus)*, Chameleon Plant *(Houttuynia cordata "Varigata")*, Primrose Creeper *(Ludwigia arcuta)*, Water Mint *(Mentha aquatica)*, Arrowhead *(Sagittaria)*, Pickerel Rush *(Pontederia)*, Bog Bean *(Menyanthes trifolia)*, Golden Club *(Orontium aquaticum)* and Marsh Fern *(Dryopteris thelypteris)*.

Although it does not produce flowers, Four-Leaf Water Clover is a lovely marginal plant.

TROPICAL OR ANNUAL MARGINALS

These plants also look lovely at the water's edge. Popular tropical or annual marginals include the following: Sensitive Plant *(Neptunia aquatica)*, Umbrella Grass *(Cyperus alternifolius)*, Water Canna *(Canna flaccida)*, Spider Lily *(Crinum Americanum)*, Common Calla *(Zantedeschia aethipica)*, Taro *(Colocasia)*, Red Monkey Flower *(Mimulus x "Lothian Fire")*, Water Blue Bell *(Ruellia brittoniana)* and Peacock Water Hyacinth *(Eichhornia azurea)*.

Sometimes it is difficult to tell whether a plant is a bog plant or a marginal plant, as many are "crossovers." For example, the aquatic Irises will do well as bog plants, or as marginals. Shallow water plants are available in hardy and tropical varieties. Again, treat the hardy types as perennials and the tropical plants as annuals. When choosing plants, it is always wise to closely read the plant tag attached to it.

Arrowhead varieties are the mainstay of the garden pond.

Black Taro has charcoal black leaves.

Underwater Plants

Another group of aquatic plants are known as "oxygenators." They are underwater plants (often referred to as "submerged" plants) that grow below the surface of the water and play a role in combating algae growth by consuming excess nutrients. They work best when planted in large clusters or groupings in the bottom of the pond. Sometimes they are tied with a string or rubber band and sometimes they are "twist-tied" with a bendable weight, which keeps the bunch together as it holds it to the bottom of the pond.

ANACHARIS (*Elodea canadensis*)

Anacharis is the most common of the underwater plants. This plant is lush and bright green, with a somewhat fernlike appearance. Fish love to forage through the dense leaves, and it is often used as an aquarium plant. Occasionally, this plant sends tiny white flowers to the surface. It is hardy to zone 5.

CABOMBA (*Cabomba*)

Cabomba provides an excellent spawning area for fish. It has fans of purple-backed foliage with green tops that are crowned with white flowers in the summer months. Cabomba is hardy to zone 6.

HORNWORT OR COONTAIL (*Ceratophyllum demersum*)

Hornwort is hardy to zone 5. This plant remains submerged and is unrooted. The bright green foliage turns almost black in winter when the plant is dormant. This plant is very easy to grow and also provides a wonderful spawning ground for fish.

Flowering Aquatics

The large flowering aquatics, Water Lilies and Lotus, are most definitely the "belles of the ball!" Large colorful blossoms provide a summer show that no other plant (aquatic or otherwise) can match.

WATER LILIES

To me, there is absolutely nothing more beautiful than a Water Lily (*Nymphaea*) floating on the surface of the garden pond. As you admire one, time almost seems to stand still—allowing you to cast aside every care from your mind as you become entranced in its grace and beauty. Almost everyone knows what a Water Lily looks like. The famous paintings of Water Lilies by the French artist Claude Monet have left an indelible imprint on the minds of many!

Although most people know what a Water Lily is, most are surprised to learn that there are hundreds of different kinds, divided into two major types: hardy and tropical.

Hardy Water Lilies

The hardy varieties of Water Lily are usually the best
choice for the entry-level pondkeeper. They are easy to
grow and overwinter in the pond without damage to
the rootstock, provided that the crown of the plant is
covered by at least 12 inches of water. There are over
250 species and cultivars of Water Lily available. Color
choices include white, red, pink, yellow, cream, peach,
changeables and bicolors. Some Water Lilies have a
spread of over 18 feet, while others will not spread
beyond 3 to 4 feet. These smaller varieties are wonderful for container gardens or where several varieties are
desired in a small pond. Some of the dwarf varieties
have blossoms no larger than a silver dollar, while others can get as large as 8 inches in diameter. In addi-

*Everyone loves
Water Lilies.*

tion to the color and
size, there are many
other differences in
the hardy Water Lily
varieties. Petal number
can range from less
than a dozen in some
cultivars to over forty
individual petals in
others. Some of the
blossoms have pointed
petals that open very
wide, making them
appear stellate or star-shaped. Others hold a tightly
"cupped" shape. Some boast a large number of petals,
so they are appropriately categorized as a "double stellate" or a "double cup." These can look somewhat like
a large peony blossom. Hardy Water Lilies like to have
their crown covered by at least 1 foot of water throughout the year. Most hardy Water Lily flowers float on
the surface of the water; however, there are those
that are supported by strong stems that can lift the
blossom several inches above the water's surface!

It is important to remember, however, that a Water
Lily is not a Water Lily is not a Water Lily! When you
select one for your pond, be sure that it has a plant

identification tag or culture card attached to it. This tag should tell you the correct name of the species (subspecies or cultivar) and the expected growing habit of the plant. Steer clear of Water Lilies that are simply labeled "Red Water Lily," or "Yellow Water Lily." You'll never know what you'll get.

Tropical Water Lilies

Tropical Water Lilies are not winter hardy and should be treated as an annual in the colder zones. There are two types of tropical Water Lilies: day-blooming and night-blooming. The night-blooming varieties begin to open about 4:00 to 5:00 p.m. and remain open until approximately 9:00 to 10:00 a.m. Many people love the night-blooming varieties, as the blossoms are just opening when they arrive home from a long day at work and can be enjoyed all evening long. Exterior pond lights really help to showcase these plants! Both the day-bloomers and the night-bloomers are gorgeous. In fact, some of the tropical varieties are so perfectly beautiful and have such vibrant coloration that some people question whether or not they are live plants! The spectacular array of colors available in tropical Water Lilies include deep purple, lavender and blue hues, magenta, deep red, burgundy, cream, white, peach, pink, salmon and even green and "almost" black. Tropical Water Lilies hold their blossoms high upon strong stems, and most varieties are profuse bloomers. Many will bloom well into the autumn months.

A hardy Water Lily is a good choice for the novice pond-keeper.

Tropical Water Lilies can be a bit more expensive than the hardy varieties, so if you live in a colder growing zone, you might want to try to overwinter the tropical Water Lilies indoors. Before the first killing frost, bring the Lily into your basement or dimly lit garage. Tropical Water Lilies all need dormancy so that they will bloom again next season. The trick is to keep them cool (but not too cold—between 45° and 55°F), in a dark or dimly lit room for the duration of winter. You can place the Lily (pot and all) in a black plastic garbage bag. Loosely fold down the bag to block out light, but so that some air gets into the bag. Do not water the Lily tuber during dormancy. Many horticulturists will take the Lily tuber out of the growing pot, rinse off the soil with water and place the tuber in a plastic bag. They then place the bag in a refrigerator set at between 45° and 55°F and let it alone for a few months. In the spring, they repot it (using fresh soil), and start it in a greenhouse. Because they are difficult to overwinter, many pondkeepers opt to treat tropical Water Lilies as annuals and dispose of them after the first frost.

Some hardy Water Lily blossoms have a "cupped" shape.

Many tropical Water Lilies are viviparous. This means that small plantlets may form at the juncture of the stem and the leaf blade during the growing season. It is possible to start new plants with these "baby" plantlets.

Tropical Water Lilies should not be placed into the pond until all threat of frost has passed and until the pond water warms to 70°F. Do not lower them to the bottom of the pond as you would with hardy Water Lilies. Place them so that the crown of the plant is covered by just a few inches of water.

Many of the hardy and tropical Water Lily varieties are scented, and all of the night-blooming varieties are scented. Like perfumes, Water Lily scents can range from captivating to overpowering. You may want to "sniff" before you buy!

LOTUS

Lotus (*Nelumbo*) have gained in popularity over the past several years. At one time, consumers were intimidated by their size, their unique flowers and charming foliage. They believed that they were much too exotic and undoubtedly much too difficult to grow. This is not the case. Lotus are very easy to grow and feel just as at home in a water-filled pot as they do in a large

A tropical night-blooming Water Lily can be spectacular!

pond. Lotus are revered in China and other Asian countries as sacred symbols. They are also used as a food source; the seeds and tubers are edible and quite nutritious. The leaves of the Lotus are round and somewhat bowl-shaped. Water beads and rolls right off the leaves, making them unique.

Many Lotus cultivars produce flowers that grow as large as 12 inches in diameter! The larger varieties can grow to over 6 feet in height. In addition to the larger varieties, there are semidwarf and dwarf varieties available. Some of the dwarf Lotus reach a maximum height of 18 inches and produce smaller, but just as beautiful, flowers. Lotus require little in care and maintenance

57

but prefer that their crown is covered by no more than 6 inches of water. Lotus can be purchased potted throughout the year or bare root in early spring. Lotus can take a while to get started, but they bloom well through the summer months—and some into early fall. Most Lotus are hardy to zone 4. They are available in pink, red, white, cream, lemon yellow and bicolor. Some of the more popular Lotus varieties include: Hindu Lotus *(Nelumbo nucifera)*, American Yellow Lotus *(Nelumbo lutea)*, Mrs. PDS *(Nelumbo "Mrs. Perry D. Slocum")*, *Nelumbo "The Queen,"* Asiatic Lotus *(Nelumbo "Alba Grandiflora")*, Empress Lotus *(Nelumbo "Alba Striata")*, Tulip Lotus *(Nelumbo nucifer "Shirokunski")*, Double Rose Lotus *(Nelumbo "Rosea Plena")* and *Nelumbo "Momo Botan."*

KEEP YOUR LOTUS PODS

When the Lotus petals fall after blooming, you will notice that the green pod remains on the stem. Leave the pods alone. They will dry and become woody. In the fall, snip the pods, stem and all, and add them to your dried flower arrangements!

Lotus are easy to grow.

LILY-LIKE AQUATICS

Another group of aquatic plants called the "Lily-likes" are darling little plants that do not require a lot of space. Their leaves float on top of the surface of the water like those of the Water Lily, and they have small delicate-looking flowers that are quite captivating.

Water Hawthorne (Aponogeton distachyus)

One of my favorite of the Lily-likes is the Water Hawthorne. It thrives in cold water and is known as the winter flowering plant because it will bloom best in the late fall and early spring. In the warmer climates, it will remain in bloom throughout the winter. So long as the water does not freeze over, the Water Hawthorne will be blooming. I have found that if you place the Water Hawthorne in the deepest part of the pond, it will continue to bloom throughout most of the summer months, too, so long as the roots and crown remain cool.

The flowers are white and very fragrant. The leaves are oblong and can range from green to red on the same plant. This plant can become invasive, however, as the blossoms turn to seed pods that drop off and seed themselves in the smallest amount of silt or even in their neighbor's pots. I have had to pull them from the

The "Momo Botan" Lotus variety works well in ponds of all sizes.

pots of my Water Lilies several times throughout the year because they make themselves such frequent uninvited guests! They seem to like moving water and will do well at the base of a waterfall or in a moving stream, so long as the current isn't too strong.

The Water Hawthorne makes a wonderful cut flower displayed in a bud vase. The blooms last several days after they have been cut, and they emit a wonderful sweet fragrance reminding you of a potted Hyacinth at Eastertime.

Other Popular Lily-likes

The Banana Lily (*Nymphoides aquatica*), Cristatum (*Nymphoides cristatum*), Geminata (*Nymphoides geminata*), Floating Heart (*Nymphoides peltata*) and Indica or Water Snowflake (*Nymphoides indica*) all have waxy floating leaves and star- or cupped-shaped blossoms. Some of the blossoms are yellow and a few are white.

If you do not have a lot of room in your pond to include a Water Lily or a Lotus, a Lily-like plant is the next best thing. They are easy to care for and are profuse bloomers adding color and interest to the pond for most of the growing season.

Growing Methods

Many entry-level pondkeepers are confused as to how plants are grown in a garden pond. In a natural or earth-bottom pond, they grow quite naturally in the soil, clay and silt at the bottom. There are many native plants that will spring up out of nowhere when the conditions become right. Birds will drop undigested seeds as they fly over the pond, where they can germinate at will. The plants may become hard to control, particularly if the pond depth is less than 3 feet. In a relatively shallow pond, the introduction of invasive species can quickly turn it into a marsh, and then into a bog. Eventually, the pond will dry up completely.

In a garden or ornamental pond, the pondkeeper can quite easily control the aquatic plant overgrowth by planting aquatic plants in no-hole plastic pots. These pots are usually black in color so they are easily disguised in the pond. The pots come in a variety of sizes and are used for marginal plants, Water Lilies and Lotus. The larger pots (8 inches and over) have built-in handle depressions that make it easy to lower the plant into the water and easy to remove the plant when it comes time to repot it. There are mesh pots on the market, but most growers do not recommend them. It is easy for soil and fertilizer to leach into the pond water from mesh pots, and roots will intertwine, making it almost impossible to remove the plant without totally destroying the basket.

POTTING AQUATIC PLANTS

Most aquatic plants available on the retail level are already potted in small pots, but will have to be repotted before you place them in the pond. If they are not repotted, the plants may not have enough room to grow and thrive.

Repotting an aquatic plant is a fairly easy procedure. Most aquatic plants are tolerant of less than perfect soil conditions. They prefer a good, substantial garden loam that has a somewhat heavy sand or clay component. Aquatic plants do not need to be planted in deep soil, so place a couple of inches of soil in the bottom of the pot. Place the plant in the new container. With the exception of Water Lilies and Lotus, place the plant in the center of the pot. Then, place one or two aquatic fertilizer tablets in the pot, but not right on top of the root mass. Cover the root mass and tablets with enough soil to cover the crown. To prevent the soil from lifting out of the pot, top the container with a shallow layer of pea gravel. This will also discourage fish from digging in the soil and disturbing the root system.

Plant your Water Lilies in no-hole plastic pots.

Saturate the newly potted plant with a hose before placing it in the pond. This will help to dispel air pockets in the soil, which, in addition to the pea gravel, will keep the soil from lifting out of the pot. When you place the pot in the pond, be sure to lower it s-l-o-w-l-y. If you just drop it into the water, the soil could explode out of the pot like a mushroom cloud, and your efforts will have been for naught.

Water Lilies and Lotus have rhizomatous root systems whereby the roots grow horizontally. A Lotus tuber looks somewhat like a banana. When you pot either of these plants, you will place the tuber next to the pot with the growing tip facing the center of the pot. This will give the tuber the entire diameter of the pot in which to grow. Do not place it in the center of the pot, as this will diminish its growing space. Use the same potting procedure as with the other aquatic plants with the exception of the placement of the root system.

Aquatic Plant Fertilizers

Like most plants, aquatic plants need to be fertilized. Slow-release aquatic plant tablets are the easiest, most efficient type of fertilizer to use. One tablet will feed the plant for three to four months, thus you need only feed the plants in the spring in the colder climates and no more than twice a year in the warmer growing zones. The fertilizer tablets are about the size of a nickel and are approximately ½-inch thick. When feeding established plants, you simply push the tablet 1 to 2 inches down into the soil. If you don't push it down far enough, the nutrients could leach into the water before the plant has a chance to absorb them, causing unpleasant algae growth.

Aquatic fertilizers come in a 10-15-10 plus micronutrient formula, which contains ten percent nitrogen, fifteen percent phosphorus, ten percent potassium and trace minerals such as copper and zinc. This formula is balanced for almost all aquatic plant needs.

A well-pruned pond will deter pests.

Maintenance of Aquatic Plants

Throughout the growing season, your plants will need occasional maintenance to keep them (and the pond) healthy and beautiful. Dead foliage and spent blossoms should be removed from the plants before they begin to decay, as these can be harmful to the fish and may cause an overabundance of algae. Using a pair of pruning shears, simply snip the dead leaves and flowers off and discard them or add them to your compost bin. A well-pruned pond will also deter pests, such as aphids, which love to feed on dying Lily pads.

AQUATIC WEEDS

No, even the pond is not safe from weeds! You may find a strange sprout of something growing in one of your aquatic plant pots and not know what it is. Aquatic weeds number in the thousands. They can come to your pond by way of seeds blowing in the wind, bird droppings containing undigested seeds or they may have been in the soil used to pot the plant. Some weeds are actually quite pretty, but can be terribly invasive. One weed in particular, known as Crisp Pondweed (*P. crispus*), has wavy, broad leaves. This weed has little brown seed spikes at the top of the plant that drop into the water and start to grow. The weed multiplies by both seed and root runners, and it can exist in depths as great as 5 feet. Once this weed is introduced to your pond, it is extremely difficult to eradicate. You may find yourself pulling weeds from the aquatic plant pots as well as the bottom of your pond where they can grow in very little soil, silt or even pea gravel.

Some of the "uninvited" seeds that germinate and grow in your pond might look somewhat weedlike, but may actually be an aquatic plant. Water Plantain (*Alisma plantagao-aquatica*) has wide, rounded leaves and a long lanky stem that shoots up through the center of the foliage cluster to form insignificant flowers. They can grow to 2 feet, including the flowering stem. Spike Rush (*Eleocharis*) can also look rather weedlike, but is actually an aquatic grass. Even Cattails can find their way to your pond. You will certainly find several unexpected surprises as you embark on your pondkeeping adventure!

THE POT-JUMPERS

Some aquatic plants are just not happy staying in their own container and try to set up shop in a neighbor's pot! I call these plants "the pot-jumpers." Plants with roots borne on creeping foliage like the Bog Bean,

Pennywort and some of the Lily-likes are known for their propensity to "repot" themselves. They trail along the water's surface until they run into another pot. Finding soil in the pot next door, they quickly lower their roots and begin to grow as a new plant. You can easily control this by keeping the creeping stems cut back so that they do not reach another pot.

chapter 5

Common Ornamental Pond Fish

Fish are wonderful additions to the garden pond. Fish provide vibrant colors and movement, and they are essential in the control of insects and some invasive plant life. Fish for ornamental purposes need to be pretty, brightly colored and fascinating to watch from  above. For this reason, most "native" fish are not good choices because their colors are somewhat dull and uninteresting. Also, native fish depend upon an well-balanced predator-to-prey fish ratio. An imbalance will result in a pond that is overrun by one species or another. Tropical "aquarium" fish are also not good choices. These fish need to be in warm temperatures at all times, and they are meant to be viewed from the side, rather than from above. Some tropical varieties may be used in ponds located in USDA zone 10, southern Florida, and zone 11, south of the mainland (see chapter 3), as temperature fluctuations are minimal and winters are very mild.

Goldfish

The majority of pondkeepers choose Goldfish (*Carassius auratus*) as their primary fish choice, and for good reasons. They are relatively inexpensive, quite hardy, brightly colored, active and people-friendly. Of the 125 varieties, some of the more popular ones include the Common Goldfish, Comet, Shubunkin, Oranda, Lionhead, Pompom, Ryukin, Pearlscale, Black Moor, Celstial, Bubble-eye and Telescope (or Telescope-eye). Not all of these fish are hardy or good selections for an outdoor pond environment. The varieties of Goldfish that are best suited to the pond environment include Common Goldfish, Comets and Shubunkin. They all have sleek bodies and are fast swimmers. They are hardy and can be overwintered in the pond in even the coldest of temperatures. In the pond environment, Goldfish can grow quite large, over 16 inches in some cases. They also breed freely in the spring and early summer months and their mating chases are quite amusing to watch.

Common Goldfish have shiny red, orange or white scales.

POPULAR GOLDFISH

There are two basic types of Goldfish: scaled and scaleless.

Common Goldfish

Common Goldfish usually have shiny red, orange or white scales; however, yellow, black and brown colors can also be found.

Comets

The Comets have colors similar to those of the Common Goldfish, but their tail (caudal) fins are exceptionally long and flowing. The tail fins are as long as the bodies on some specimens. Comets add an elegant touch to the pond and are just as hardy as the Common Goldfish.

Shubunkin

The Shubunkin have scales that are transparent, and so are generally thought of as "scaleless." They are especially beautiful. Their bodies are a silver-blue or blue-gray color, which is usually mottled with red,

The Calico Shunbunkin is exceptionally beautiful.

white, black or chocolate brown coloration. The Shubunkin are a calico (three color) fish with exceptionally attractive markings. Shubunkin were developed by the Japanese almost 100 years ago. There are two varieties of Shubunkin, the Bristol and the London. The London is almost identical to the Common Goldfish, with the exception of its coloration. The Bristol is similar to the London in its body shape, but it boasts an enormously beautiful tail fin. The Bristol's tail fin is wide, rather than long like the tail of the Comet. The value of a particular Shubunkin specimen is increased by the depth of its blue color.

Fancy Goldfish

Fancy Goldfish with rounded, full bodies and double tail fins, and those with telescopic or bubble-eyes,

Orandas and Black Moors, can be kept in a garden pond during the summer months in the colder zones, but should be moved to an indoor aquarium in the winter. In the warmer zones, they can be kept in the pond throughout the year.

Although beautiful to watch, with their large, egg-shaped bodies and flowing tails, the Goldfish in the "fancy" category do not tend to thrive in an outdoor pond environment. They are a more delicate fish, and their round bodies make it difficult for them to swim and escape predators. They do not adjust well to temperature changes and the normal day-to-night temperature fluctuation can be enough to stress them.

These fish can be separated into two basic groups: those with and those without a dorsal fin (the fin on the top of the body). Those varieties without a dorsal fin, such as the Celestial, Pompom, Lionhead and Bubble-eye, have a particularly difficult time swimming. They seem to wiggle their way through the water, gaining just an inch at a time. Those with dorsal fins, including the Fantail, Oranda, Veiltail Ryukin, Black Moor and Telescope, can swim more easily and are a prettier fish to watch.

Fancy Goldfish tend to develop dropsy and swim bladder disease. Dropsy is an ailment that is most commonly fatal. The fish seems to swim in a disoriented fashion—sideways, upside down, even floating on the top. The scales puff outward, giving it a pinecone appearance. It is not known exactly what causes dropsy or how to cure it.

Swim bladder disease is caused by constipation. The swim bladder is an internal organ that gives the fish buoyancy, allowing it to remain afloat. It is a gas-filled sac that is located inside the body above the fish's other internal organs. The sac in most fish is single and elongated, but in the Goldfish it is divided into two parts. In the flat-bodied Goldfish, like the Common Goldfish, Comet and Shubunkin, the sacs are of equal size. However, in the fancy varieties, the sacs are globe-shaped, with the sac in the front being much smaller than the one in the rear. The disparity in sac size causes a slight bobbing as the fish swims, usually with its head downward. With the unusual shapes in the fancy varieties caused by hybridization, the intestinal tracts and other internal organs are not in normal alignment, making the fish more susceptible to constipation and resulting disease. When the fish becomes constipated, bacterial infection results, which in turn can cause the buildup of fluids and gases in the body cavity. Unfortunately, there is little that can be done to treat this ailment.

Fancy Goldfish like this Oranda are more delicate than Common Goldfish varieties.

No matter what the variety, all Goldfish will interbreed in the pond, and in just a few short years, the mongrel fish will all look alike. Note that it can take up to two years for a Goldfish to show its true colors. They may appear one color as juveniles, changing to an entirely different color and/or pattern as adults.

If you want to breed your fish to be true to their variety, you must prevent random matings from occurring or remove the mixed breed fish to prevent them from breeding, too. This may be difficult, and you may find it more of a bother than it is worth.

Koi

Nishikigoi (more commonly called Koi) are the king fish of the pond. They are a large, bold and muscular fish that will require a lot of room if they are to develop appropriately. Although you may buy them when they are just a few inches long, they will quickly grow to over 1 foot and eventually to over 2 feet! Although there are some exceptions reported, Koi really do not belong in a water garden. They can be quite destructive to aquatic plants, sometimes completely uprooting them and shredding Water Lilies to coleslaw!

There are two groups of pondkeepers really; water gardeners and "Koikeepers." Koikeepers are typically not water gardeners. Koi are the reason they have a pond, rather than acquiring a Koi because they have a pond. Collectors have been known to spend tens of thou-

*Koi are large,
muscular fish.*

sands of dollars for one champion quality Koi! The majority of Koi enthusiasts have little desire to have a gorgeous display of aquatic plant life. This is a personal decision, and many people will discover early on where their loyalties will lie. There are ways to compromise, of course, so your Koi can live in harmony with their aquatic counterparts. You can protect your plant pots with Koi-proof mesh container covers and segregate the floating plants from the Koi with the use of plant protectors.

If one is to keep Koi exclusively, however, special filtration methods will have to be practiced carefully to maintain a healthy environment for the Koi, which produce a lot of waste. Ultraviolet sterilizers are one way of helping to keep the water clear, as the vast amount of organic waste produced by Koi cause algae to bloom excessively.

Koi are dramatically beautiful with shiny scales of iridescent colors and patterns that bedazzle their human audience. Some flaunt metallic scales that glimmer and sparkle in the sunshine. Although Koi look somewhat like Goldfish, the barbels on their mouths set them apart. The barbels resemble those of Catfish, and are quite apparent when they come to the surface to feed on the tidbits with which their owners indulge them.

Koi were developed by the Japanese. The earliest references to the colored Carp date back as far as the sixth century A.D. *Cyrpinus Carpio,* the common Carp from which the Koi was derived, is a very plain fish that was grown for food in Japan in the early seventeenth century. The villagers who raised this fish would occasionally find an especially colorful specimen and begin to selectively breed them. As the color patterns were stabilized, the Japanese began to call this fish "Nishikigoi," which means brocaded Carp. They are long-lived, and with proper conditions can live thirty years or more. There are documented cases of Koi living over 200 years! They are very friendly and can be taught to willingly eat from their owner's hand.

Long-finned or Butterfly Koi can be extremely lovely. They have the large, massive bodies, distinctive barbels and the wonderfully extravagant colors of the standard Koi, but they also have long, flowing fins to put icing on the cake! They are striking additions to the pond.

KOI COLORS

Entire books have been written on the Koi and justifiably so. There is much to learn about them. One of the most fascinating aspects of the Koi is their many color combinations and patterns. The color varieties are named in Japanese, and it takes quite a while to learn all of the color varieties. For example,

---

THE VARIETY OF KOI

Here are just some of the Koi delineations:

Aka: Red

Budo: Grape

Doitsu: Scaleless

Gin: Silver

Go-shiki: Five colors

Haku: White

Hi: Red

Hikari: Metallic

Kanoko: Fawn-dappled

Ki: Yellow

Kin: Gold

Kujaku: Peacock

Muji: Solid

Ogon: Gold

Rin: Scales

Sanke: Three colors

Shiro: White

Sumi: Black

Utsuri: Reflection

Yamabuki: Yellow

Now, can you determine what a Gin Rin Tancho would look like? If you said a silver-scaled fish with a round red spot on its head, you would be correct!

a Kohaku is a white fish with a red pattern. A Sanke is a Kohaku with black spots. A Showa is a Kohaku with black bands around the body. A Tancho is a fish with a round red spot on its head with no other red on the body. It may be white or black and white. Some varieties have larger-than-life names like Yamatonishiki, which is a metallic Sanke.

Although beautiful and fascinating, remember that Koi need a deep, large pond. If your pond is to be small and less than 3 feet deep, it is probably best to keep fish other than Koi.

The varieties of Koi seem almost endless.

Golden Orfe (*Leuciscus idus*)

One of the most underrated fish is the Golden Orfe. This little speed demon is constantly on the go. It likes to cruise the surface of the pond in shoals, or schools, in search of insects or other tasty tidbits. Golden Orfe are colorful members of the Trout family, but they are a calm and peaceful fish, making them quite compatible with Goldfish and Koi. They are delightful to watch, as they will jump slightly above the water's surface to catch insects in flight, and for this reason may sometimes jump out of the pond. They can at times flip themselves back into the water, so long as the rim of the pond is level with the water. These slender, torpedo-shaped, salmon-colored fish usually have a small brown dot or speckles on their head. They can reach a length of more than 1 foot in ideal conditions, and do best in ponds that are at least 5 to 6 feet in diameter. In some states with warmer climates, Golden Orfe cannot be imported. This ban prevents them from escaping and from being introduced into natural waterways where they would compete with the natural game fish for food.

Golden Orfe are winter-hardy in most parts of the country and grow quite rapidly. As they get older, their colors deepen from a light, bronzelike gold to a brilliant gold.

Rosy Gold Minnow (*Pimephales promelas*)

The Rosy Gold Minnow is a color variety of the common Fathead Minnow. These are small fish growing to about 2½ inches in length. Their small size makes them an excellent choice for smaller ponds. They are very hardy and breed prolifically, usually many times throughout the summer. The eggs are laid on the undersides of floating objects, including Water Lily pads. They are not cannibalistic if provided with enough to eat. Rosy Gold Minnows are tolerant of less than ideal water conditions, as long as extreme pH or hardness values are avoided. They thrive on mosquito larvae and happily take processed flake food to supplement their appetite. Because of their bright rosy color, they have been bred as bait fish and millions are also sold as "feeder fish" in some areas of the country. To buy these fish at a very small price, simply visit a bait shop. Don't get too attached to them, however—Rosy Golds usually do not live much longer than two years, but their offspring should continue to replenish perpetually.

> **AVOID STOCKING YOUR POND WITH CHANNEL CATFISH**
>
> It is advisable to stay away from Channel Catfish (including the albino) varieties. They are voracious night feeders that may rip and tear the fins and eyes of your prized pond fish to bits. There are cases where they have lived quite hospitably with Koi and larger Goldfish, but too often they attack the smaller, slower and weaker specimens.

Tench (*Tinca tinca*)

There are two species of Tench available for the garden pond: the Golden Tench and the Wild or "Green" Tench. Tench are bottom feeders and love to rummage around for a meal. Their foragings can stir up the pond bottom if it is dirty. On the other hand, they can be good pond additions in that they will eat the leftovers that surface feeders may let fall to the bottom. Tench grow a little larger than 1 foot in an ornamental pond, although they can obtain a length of 2 feet in the wild. They are attractive fish that are usually a light golden color.

There are several other suitable pond fish choices to be considered. Check to see what varieties are available in your area.

What Gives Fish Their Unique Coloration?

The same pigments responsible for the orange color in carrots, the yellow in marigolds and the red in red bell peppers are responsible for the bright coloration of fish and other animals. These pigments are called carotenoids, but only plants and microorganisms are capable of de novo synthesis. In fish, body colors are the result of specialized cells in the skin called chromatophores, which contain colored pigments such as carotenoids.

Fish, like other animals, are unable to synthesize carotenoids, so they must obtain these pigments from their diet. Natural food organisms will provide carotenoids to fish through the food chain (for example, fish will eat the worms or invertebrates that have eaten algae and plankton that contain carotenoids).

Because most ornamental ponds do not have enough natural foods for fish to obtain the right amount of carotenoids, they are available in manufactured fish foods. Some of these packaged foods will even state "color enhancers added" on the label, which means that carotenoids are included.

Choosing Fish for the Pond

In addition to the right variety of fish for your particular garden pond, you will want to make sure that the individual fish you choose is healthy and free of parasites and disease. Buy from a respectable pet shop or water garden retailer with a reputation for supplying good quality fish. Ask how long the fish has been in their store. Fish tend to experience stress during shipment, and the mortality rate can be high. Choose fish that have been in the store for more than a few days. Also, it can take as long as 2 weeks for some diseases and parasite symptoms to show up on the fish. For this reason, the longer the fish has been in the location you are buying from, the better chance you have of getting a healthy fish. If a particular fish has caught your eye, inspect it carefully all over. If you notice any signs of sore spots, fungus (which appears as a white powdery puff), parasites or lethargy, do not buy the fish. Also, if the fish seems to display erratic behavior, thrashing itself against the sides or bottom of the tank, it could have parasites.

If a particular color of fish attracts your attention, you should know that the fish's color will probably change as it matures. Sometimes Goldfish can be a lovely shade of bronze as youngsters, but then turn to a bright red or even red and white as they mature. If you are set on a particular color of fish, you should buy a mature fish that has its permanent color in place.

Getting the Pond Ready for Fish

Before stocking your pond with fish, you will want to make sure that the water quality is conducive to their health and survival. It is wise to first stock the pond with the aquatic plants. Tiny, tender plants will need time to develop, and they can be harmed when the fish nibble at their leaves. The plants will give the fish a place to hide and to forage. The plants will also help to protect the fish from direct sun. After the plants have been in the pond for about a week, you should test the pH of the pond water. Using an inexpensive and simple to use pH test kit (available at most pet stores), test the water. If the pH level is between 6.5 and 8.5, your pond is usually safe for fish. An ideal reading is between 7.0 and 7.5. If the test reads over 8.5, the water is alkaline and will need to be treated to bring the level down. You will also need to find the reason for the high pH reading. A reading over 8.5 could indicate the presence of lime in the water, which could come from dissolved concrete if you used mortar, or from concrete blocks in the water.

Bringing the Fish Home

After you have selected the fish for your garden pond, you will need to take care in transporting them and acclimating them to their new home. Fish are usually netted and placed in heavy plastic bags with enough water and air to keep them alive until they reach their final destination. It is advisable that you set the bag upright in a cardboard box or container to give the

Float the plastic bag in the pond for about fifteen to twenty minutes before releasing the fish.

fish enough water depth and to prevent excess movement during transportation.

When you get the fish home, float the plastic bag in the pond for fifteen or twenty minutes to allow the water temperature in the bag to stabilize with that of the pond water. If it is a hot, sunny day, you should put a white or light-colored towel or rag over the top of the bag to deflect the sun's rays, which can heat the water in the bag to dangerously high temperatures.

After the water in the bag has warmed or cooled to the pond water temperature, remove about the same amount of pond water that is in the bag from the pond and place it in a bucket. Then, gently release the fish (along with the water in the bag) into the bucket. Slowly add a little more pond water to the bucket over a five- to ten-minute period to acclimate the fish. Then, using a net, remove the fish from the bucket and slowly release the fish into the pond. Do not put the water in the bucket back into the pond. The reasons for following this procedure are, obviously, to slowly acclimate the fish to the pond water and to reduce the possibility of shock. By doing so, you will also avoid introducing any harmful organisms that may be present in the fish's water.

To be completely safe, you may choose to quarantine and medicate the new fish in a separate holding container for 2 weeks and watch for signs of illness. The incubation period for most disease is no longer than 2 weeks, so if your fish are healthy after the quarantine period has passed, it will be safe to introduce them to the pond. There is always some risk of introducing disease, fungus and/or parasites when adding a new fish to the garden pond. If the pond is small, you may choose to disinfect it entirely with specially formulated medication. You will want to be sure that the medicine recommended by the fish store will not harm your aquatic plants or other pond inhabitants before using it.

Feeding and Caring for Pond Fish

Feeding fish in the garden pond is one of the most enjoyable parts of owning a backyard pond. The fish will soon begin to recognize you and will rush to the pond's edge to welcome you as they greedily accept the food that you offer them. Fish food comes in flake, stick or pellet form. The flake form is used primarily for Goldfish and the smaller pond fishes, while the more substantial pellets or sticks are manufactured for the larger Koi. The processed fish food on the market is of good quality. Most brands are supplemented with the vitamins and minerals essential to a fish's development. The key is to not overfeed. While it is enjoyable to see the fishes scramble to you when you appear at the pond's edge, don't be taken in by their friendly charm and begin to feed them every time! This overfeeding practice could lead to a high level of organic waste in the pond that will ultimately prove to be too great a load for your filtration system to handle; the fish will become ill and could die.

In the summer, when the fish are active, feed them about once a day. Only give them as much as they can consume within a five-minute period. In the autumn (in the cooler climates), as the water cools, the fish will become increasingly inactive and begin to refuse food. When this happens, discontinue feedings until spring. In the spring, the water temperature has to warm to at least 50°F before the fish will become interested in food. At this time, you will want to start feeding with a low-protein mix until the water temperature reaches 65°F, when you should begin feeding a high-protein formula. Continue feeding the high-protein mix for the duration of the summer. In the fall, when the water temperature cools to 60°F, begin to feed the low-protein formula until they refuse to eat.

Feeding your pond fish is fun, but don't overdo it.

Do not feed at all during the winter months, unless you are located in the warmer parts of the U.S. where the fish are active throughout the year. Most fish food companies now manufacture low-protein and high-protein feeds.

Spawning

Pond fish are promiscuous breeders and will spawn at will, usually in the spring and throughout the summer months. Their mating rituals are quite amusing to watch.

Goldfish, Golden Orfes, Rosy Gold Minnows and Koi are all egg layers. They prefer to lay their eggs on plants or solid objects within the pond. When the water warms to over 65°F and the fish are ripe with eggs, the courtship rituals will begin. You will notice males chasing the females throughout the pond. During this three- to seven-day period, the colors of both genders intensify. The males will then pursue forcefully, driving the females into plants. The males are relentless in their determination to breed.

After several hours of constant pursuit, spawning begins. The actual mating involves the pair gyrating from side to side as the male continues to push the female into the plants. During these movements, eggs and sperm are ejected into the water and adhere to the plants by sticky strings. The pair will repeat this process several times, taking brief interludes to gobble up as many of the eggs as they can. Spawning can last for a few hours.

> ### FISH IN YOUR FILTER
>
> When you notice baby fish swimming in your pond, you can bet some will find their way into the filtration system. You may want to check the filter often during this developmental time, releasing any babies that may be found back into the pond.

Afterwards, the pair (as well as other fish in the pond) will consume as many of the eggs as they can find. While a Goldfish can lay thousands of eggs during one spawning, most will be eaten by their cannibalistic parents and other pond inhabitants. A few eggs will survive and thus achieve adulthood.

Goldfish eggs look like little transparent balls. You may notice tiny black spots within the eggs, which are the eyes. They become more prevalent as the embryos develop. Incubation requires five to eight days, depending on the temperature of the water. The warmer the water, the faster the eggs will develop. As the eggs come close to their hatching time, you will notice the baby fish wiggling about inside the eggs. The eggs will then hatch, with the tail emerging first. The baby fish hang on to plants, the sides of the pond or rocks, with glands that they have in their heads. This period lasts for two days, after which time they release themselves and begin to swim in search for food and shelter.

Baby fish feed on the microscopic plant and animal life found in algae. You may supplement their diets by giving them finely powdered foods available at most pet and aquarium stores. They also love the live or frozen food you can find there, such as microworms or baby brine shrimp.

Recognizing Diseased or Injured Fish

Even a fish that has been in the pond for a long time may develop an ailment or become injured. Unless several fish are affected, it is always better to remove and treat the fish rather that treat the entire pond. Remove a bucketful of pond water. Net the ill or injured fish and place it in the quarantine bucket. You can use the bucket as a temporary "hospital" where you medicate the fish while keeping it safely away from the other pond fish. Of course, if the fish is too large for a bucket, a larger container or aquarium must be used.

There are many products on the market to treat various ailments. To treat a fish, you will need to know how to recognize when a fish is in distress. Here are some indicators that a fish is sick or injured:

- It is floating sideways or upside down or is laying at the bottom of the pond for long periods.
- It looks puffy or the scales are sticking out, making it appear like a pinecone.
- It has a red sore(s) or ulcer(s) on its body.
- It has bloody streaks through its tail or fins.
- It is "flashing" or ramming its body sideways into the bottom or sides of the pond.
- It has a cottonlike growth on its tail or fins.
- It has white spots on its body or other visible parasites or growths.
- It has difficulty opening and closing its gills.
- The gill area is red or bloody.
- It is refusing to eat while the others feed normally.
- It is struggling for air at the surface of the water.

If you notice any of these signs or any other abnormalities, you should quarantine the fish and seek treatment. After closely inspecting the fish, write down the symptoms you have observed and take these to the pet shop or fish retailer, where they will be able to help you diagnose the ailment and recommend the proper treatment.

Note that the mating ritual itself is very stressing and exhausting to both males and females. They may become injured if the male pushes the female into a jagged rock or other object. You'll want to check both after spawning.

chapter 6

Frogs
and Other **Pond**
Inhabitants

If you build it, they will come! This is a surprisingly true statement. Most new pondkeepers feel compelled to capture a frog from a wild pond or buy tadpoles and snails from the pet shop with which to stock their new pond, only to find that they will move on and others will come. In addition to fish, frogs, snails, toads, turtles, Water Snakes, crayfish, newts and other aquatic critters will find their way to your pond. Where do they come from and how do they know that you have a pond? These are questions that only Mother Nature can answer, but you can be sure that they will come and make themselves right at home. They are enjoyable to watch and listen to and you may find yourself giving them all names, like you might do with your fish!

From time to time you may notice a small new fish or two in the pond that didn't seem to be there the day before. You may wonder if the neighbor had emptied his Goldfish bowl into your pond when he grew tired of caring for it! This is probably not the case at all. It is more likely that you brought a new aquatic plant home that had some fish eggs or hatchlings attached to it, and when you placed the plant in your pond, the fish were introduced to their new home. This occurs quite often, and it is exciting to watch them develop to find out what species of fish you have acquired. (We all hope and fantasize that it will grow to be a grand champion Koi that we can cash in for about $10,000 some day. You'll have better luck playing the lottery!)

Frogs

Frogs are the acrobats of the pond. They leap and splash and blurt out amusing croaks and noises via balloonlike vocal sacs. Their antics make us smile and giggle in sheer delight! There are many varieties of frogs native throughout the U.S. Frogs can be divided into three major groups: Green Frogs, Brown Frogs and Stream Frogs. The Green Frogs are largely aquatic and are those most likely to invite themselves to your pond. In the U.S., the most common members of the Green Frog category include American Bullfrogs (*Rana catesbeiana*), American Green Frogs (*Rana clamitans melanota*) and Leopard Frogs (*Rana pipiens*). Although the group is called Green Frogs, they can come in a variety of green and brownish shades. You may, on occasion, be lucky enough to spot an albino frog, which is yellow with reddish eyes. Most Green Frogs overwinter in the water. You may, of course, find a variety of different frogs in or around your pond at some time. There are hundreds of varieties to be found across the U.S. We will address the most common species that you are likely to find in your pond. With a few exceptions, most frogs are relatively harmless and will live in complete harmony with the other creatures in the pond.

Frogs play a vital role in the control of insects and their larvae. They consume vast quantities of insects in

a single day. They are enjoyable to watch and to listen
to. Frogs will come to your garden pond on their own,
if you provide them with a habitat that is conducive to
their needs.

THE AMERICAN BULLFROG
(*Rana catesbeiana*)

Pondkeepers should beware of the American Bullfrog.
The Bullfrog, the largest North American frog, can be
found in almost every part of the United States and in
the southernmost parts of Canada. They grow to be
quite large—up to 8 inches long—and that's excluding
the legs! When outstretched they
can measure 18 inches or more!
They are green or brown in color,
with dark spots or blotches. Their
undersides are creamy white, often
mottled with a light brown. The
throat of the male may have a wash
of yellow.

**TAKE CARE WHEN
HANDLING FROGS**

Frogs and toads may harbor
microorganisms that are infectious
to humans. These include *Myco-
bacterium mariunum*, *Salmonella*
and *E. coli*. It is best to handle frogs
with disposable surgical gloves. It
is even better not to handle them at
all. Frogs have very sensitive, frag-
ile skin, and are easily injured. If
anyone picks up a frog, he or she
immediately should wash his or
her hands thoroughly with a
strong soap.

The Bullfrog is distinguished from
the similar-looking American Green
Frog by the absence of ridges,
called dorsolateral folds, down
either side of its back. The hind
feet are webbed, but the longest toe
protrudes beyond the webbing.
The male of this species has a large, round, external
eardrum, called a tympanum. They are true carnivores
and will devour anything that they can get into their
mouths, including mice, other frogs, tadpoles, salamanders, small birds and your prized fish. Their croak
is rather loud, deep, throaty and sounds like "jug-
o-rum, jug-o-rum." Unfortunately, many pet shops sell
tadpoles for the pond without identifying the species
of frog that they will become. Bullfrog tadpoles are
olive green in color on their backs and sides. The
plump body and narrowing paddlelike tail are dotted
with little, darker spots with sharply defined edges.
Most of these tadpoles are, in fact, Bullfrogs, and
should not be purchased for the pond.

The males are territorial and call in the evening to attract potential mates. This usually occurs from late May into mid-July. The eggs are laid in masses that resemble a disc-shaped film. A large female can lay as many as 20,000 eggs that will hatch in approximately four days, depending on the water temperature.

It takes Bullfrogs and Green Frogs up to two years (some Bullfrogs take up to three years) to completely metamorphose from tadpole to frog. They reach sexual maturity two to four years after transformation has been completed. In the wild, Bullfrogs can live for as long as eight or nine years. The record life span in captivity is sixteen years.

Bullfrogs are mostly nocturnal, and you probably won't see very much of them during the daylight hours. They become active in the evening when they feed and mate. They also love rainy evenings when they lounge by the water's edge in anticipation of a meal to pass by.

American Bullfrogs won't hesitate to consume other pond residents.

It is relatively easy to catch Bullfrogs in the evening by shining a flashlight in their eyes, (which seems to hypnotize them), and by netting them with a large fish net. If you catch a Bullfrog, take it as far away from your pond as possible—at least several miles to another pond or lake—as Bullfrogs have traveled a mile or more to find their way back to their claimed territory!

THE AMERICAN GREEN FROG
(Rana clamitans melanota)

The American Green Frog is quite common around ornamental garden ponds. This frog is widely distributed east of the Mississippi, but may also be found in Texas and Canada. They are mostly nocturnal, but love to bask on top of Lily pads and at the pond's edge during sunny days. Some get used to seeing humans and will tolerate their presence. Some will allow humans to catch them fairly easily, but they welcome a speedy release! They may be green or brown in color with a white spotted underside. The male of the species has a yellow throat and a large external eardrum like that of the Bullfrog. On occasion, you will find an American Green Frog with a bright green head and olive-colored body. There are two ridges, or dorsolateral folds, that extend from the eardrum two-thirds the distance to the hind legs. Their tympanum (eardrum) is external, and in the male it is larger than the eye, but in the female it is about the same size as the eye. They grow to 4 inches in length and, like the Bullfrog, take two years to transform from tadpole to frog. They will start calling in May, and continue through July. Their call is like that of a loose banjo string. When startled, Green Frogs will give a high-pitched "eeeep" call as they jump into the pond. They are also quite territorial and need to make their homes in permanent ponds. During rainy or wet periods, they will travel on land to new habitat areas. They hibernate in the bottom of the pond during the winter months, usually emerging in March or April. During the breeding period, the eggs are laid in jellylike masses that float on the water's surface—usually in a potted plant. It takes from three to five days for the approximately 4,000 eggs to hatch. Green Frog tadpoles are olive green on the back and sides.

American Green Frogs are pleasant pond residents.

The body and tail are spotted with black marks that have indistinct margins that fade into the background color.

Green Frogs eat insects, both those that fly near the surface of the water and those that live in the water. They can live from eight to ten years in the wild.

LEOPARD FROG (*Rana pipiens*)

The Leopard Frog gets it name from the leopardlike round to oval, lightly-edged spots that are randomly distributed over its entire body and legs. The inside of the thigh is pure white. It reaches from 3 to 5 inches in length when mature. Like the Green Frog, the Leopard Frog has the two dorsolateral folds that start at the eye and run down the back to the top of the back legs.

Leopardlike spots give the Leopard Frog its name.

The Leopard Frog often leaves the pond after the breeding season has passed and wanders in meadows or grassy fields away from the water. For this reason they are sometimes referred to as "meadow" or "grass" frogs. Its call sounds like a low snore followed by two or three clucks. They feed primarily on insects.

Like the Green Frog, the Leopard Frog lays its eggs in the spring. The egg mass, laid among vegetation in the water, can consist of up to 6,000 eggs.

The Leopard Frog can be found in the northernmost parts of Canada and in all of the United States with the exception of the tropical and arid areas. There is actually more than one kind of Leopard Frog native to the U.S.; the Southern Leopard Frog lives in the east and southeast and the Northern Leopard Frog lives in the north and Canada.

Toads

In comparison with frogs, the skin of toads feels dry and bumpy (or warty) to the touch. Glands in toads' skin are heavily distributed over the back and sides and are most concentrated in the back of the animal's head. In some species of toad, these glands can produce toxins known as bufotoxin, which makes the toad taste quite bad to predators. Care should be taken in handling toads, and hands should be washed thoroughly after picking up a toad. Contrary to myth, handling a toad will not cause warts.

Although most toads are nocturnal land-dwellers, hiding during the day under logs, rocks, in drainage pipes and in burrows, newly metamorphosed juveniles are generally active during the day. Toads will make their way into the pond to breed in the spring, with the males arriving first and calling to the females. They call to the females by inflating the vocal sacs located under their throat. When calling, the sacs will look like large balloons. The call of each species is different. Unlike frogs, most toads lay their eggs in strings rather than masses. The breeding period may go on for several weeks. Breeding is intense during this period, and the unpaired amorous males may try to breed with mating pairs, other male toads, frogs, fish or even driftwood. You may be able to identify the sex of a toad in your pond by its size: Males are usually significantly smaller than the females.

AMERICAN TOADS (*Bufo americanus*)

The American Toad is one of the most common of all toads to be found in the U.S. It may appear brown, gray or black in color with one or two large warts located within the dark spots on its back. The color of the American Toad has been known to change during stress, temperature fluctuations or humidity. The underside of the toad is white with darker blotches.

American Toads feed on insects including moths and flies, worms, slugs, beetles and crickets. They can be found almost anywhere there is water and a good source of food.

The mating call of the American Toad is probably the most beautiful and distinctive of all the members of the *Bufo* family. Its long, musical trill may go on endlessly for hours early in spring. Although they call

primarily in the evening, they will often call into the daylight hours. Dozens of males may join in, each one with a different pitch. The eggs are laid in jellylike strings that are strewn around vegetation. A single female can lay as many as 15,000 eggs. The strings soon hydrate and plump. The eggs hatch between four and fourteen days, depending

The American Toad will call for hours in the springtime.

upon the water temperature, releasing tiny black tadpoles. The tadpoles then feed in voracious schools for one to two months before transforming into tiny, completely transformed babies called toadlets. The toadlets immediately leave the pond in search of food and shelter. The American Toad grows to about 3½ inches and reaches sexual maturity in two to three years. It hibernates in the winter.

WOODHOUSE'S TOAD (*Bufo woodhousei woodhousei*)

This toad may appear a greenish-gray or golden-yellow color. It has three or more large "warts" within the dark spots found on its back. It has a light stripe down the midline. The underside is washed in yellow. It is very similar to the American Toad in most of its habits; however, its mating call is like that of a bleating sheep.

Turtles

There are many varieties of aquatic turtles native to the waters of North America. Should you introduce them to your garden pond? They are cute and captivating,

89

but they can be a challenge to keep as pond pets. Unlike fish, and even frogs, turtles will almost always escape. If you really want turtles in your pond, you must build it to be escape-proof. This means an inaccessible ledge will have to be placed around the perimeter of the pond. Turtles also need a basking site to regulate their body temperature (thermoregulation) and to prevent the development of fungal skin diseases. You will have to build an island in the middle of the pond or anchor a piece of driftwood, so the turtle(s) can get out of the water and bask in the sun for several hours a day.

If you would like turtles to live in your pond, concrete foundations and basking sites made of concrete should be avoided. The concrete will cause the turtles to suffer abraded plastrons (the bottom of their shell) and sore feet. These ailments could promote infection or disease. EPDM rubber and the rigid HDPE preformed ponds make good choices as liner materials when turtles are desired.

Install a rubber or rigid pre- formed pond if you would like to keep turtles.

Turtles may be classified as carnivorous (eating mostly animal substances), omnivorous (eating both animal and vegetable substances) or herbivorous (surviving strictly on vegetation). In some turtle species, the hatchlings and juveniles will be primarily omnivorous but later become strict vegetarians. With this in mind, you should expect turtles to eat your aquatic plants. In fact, depending on the species and its size, a turtle can do some serious damage to your Water Lilies and other water garden plants. You should also expect that some turtles will eat small fish and tadpoles. If you want to keep turtles nonetheless, you will have to find creative ways of keeping them away from the foliage and the baby fish.

Aquatic turtles feed in the water and need to be completely immersed in the water to eat. It is common for aquatic turtles to develop vitamin and mineral deficiencies if their nutritional requirements are not met. Calcium is especially important to juvenile turtles as it is essential for good shell and bone development. To supplement their diet, you may give them a manufactured food, such as ReptoMin® floating food sticks. These sticks contain all the essential ingredients for a balanced diet, and turtles (as well as newts) love them!

Should you decide to introduce turtles to your pond, you should know that they will hibernate in the winter. You must not allow the pond to freeze over, so it is advisable to purchase a small pond heater or deicer for this purpose. You must make sure that the turtles have soil-filled pots (like those you use for plants) to burrow in. These pots should be placed in the bottom of the pond. Although they can hibernate in Water Lily pots, turtles may harm or destroy the rhizome, and should be provided with plant-free pots.

One of the most popular species of aquatic turtles is the Red-Eared Slider (*Trachemys scripta*). They are commonly known as dimestore turtles, as millions of them were bred and sold in the "Five and Ten stores" during the 1960s. (Remember the plastic turtle dishes complete with basking site and fake palm tree?) Because of the threat of *Salmonella* poisoning caused by these hatchling turtles, a federal regulation was enacted prohibiting the retail sale of all turtles with a carapace (shell) length of less than 4 inches. Nearly all reptile and amphibian species can be carriers of the *Salmonella* bacteria. It is advisable to always wash your hands with an antibacterial soap immediately after handling turtles. Young children, elderly people and people with immunity deficiencies should be especially mindful of this, as they are particularly vulnerable to contracting the bacteria. It is best to keep these high-risk people away from reptiles and amphibians.

It is not illegal to own turtles less than 4 inches long; however, it *is* illegal to sell them. If you wish to catch wild native turtles to put in your pond, be sure you have permission to do so, and that you know what species the turtle is and what its eating habits are. It is probably best to obtain your turtle from a captive breeder or pet store—taking turtles from the wild can have a negative impact on the turtles' habitat. Some popular turtle choices include the following.

MAP TURTLES (*Graptemys*)

Map Turtles are carnivorous. The females grow from 7 to 10 inches in length, while the males obtain a length of 4 to 6 inches.

Painted Turtles are a nice addition to the pond and are easy to keep.

SLIDERS (*Trachemys*)

Red-Eared Sliders are native to the southeastern part of the United States. They are omnivorous, and grow to lengths of 5 to 8 inches. Young Red-Eared Sliders are a bright green color with red and yellow markings. As they mature, they become a dark olive green.

PAINTED TURTLES (*Chrysemys picta*)

Painted Turtles are not as widely available as the Sliders, but they are inexpensive and easy to keep. They are an omnivorous species that grow from 4 to 7 inches long. Painted Turtles have red and yellow stripes on an olive green background.

MUSK TURTLES (*Sternotherus*)

Musk Turtles are carnivorous turtles that grow to only 3 to 5 inches. In spite of their small size, they are aggressive little turtles and are likely to snap at fingers. They are one of the few species that can survive completely underwater.

MUD TURTLES (*Kinoesternon*)

These turtles are similar to the Musk Turtles, but may grow to be a bit larger. They, too, are carnivorous.

SNAPPING TURTLES (*Chelydra*)

One of the most dangerous turtles to have in your pond is the Snapping Turtle. They are unattractive, extremely destructive to plants and pond life and can be harmful to people. Their powerful mouths have been known to take off fingers and inflict serious bites to legs and feet. They are voracious carnivores that lie in wait with their mouths open in hopes of attracting an unsuspecting fish with their wiggly, wormlike tongue. They are very aggressive and should be removed at once if they should make their way to your garden pond.

Salamanders and Newts

Salamanders and newts are the collective name for about 320 species of amphibians having tails. They belong to the order *Urodela*. Salamanders usually live their adult lives as terrestrials, returning to the water to breed. Newts, on the other hand, are primarily aquatic. Newts may live part of their lives on land and may form a warty skin when out of water. Salamanders and newts are not lizards as some may believe. Lizards are reptiles, have dry, scaly skin, claws and external ears. Both salamanders and newts spend most of the daylight hours hiding under rocks or decaying logs. They breed and forage for food in the evening. They eat a variety of small insects, larvae, small snails, crustaceans and even fish eggs and fry.

SALAMANDERS (*Caudata*)

Salamanders are very sensitive to desiccation and are almost always found in damp areas near streams or marshlands, where they can remain wet. Salamanders may live around ponds so long as there is shade and plenty of suitable rocky hiding places. Salamanders may be very bright in color and often spotted, or striped. Many grow from 4 to 6 inches in length or more. The skin contains several glands, which may secrete moisture to help keep their skin moist. Some secrete a toxic substance that is distasteful to predators.

Newts like to be near water, and may take up residence in your pond.

Salamanders have short bodies with rounded tails, full, rounded heads and large mouths and eyes.

Should salamanders come on their own to your garden pond, you should consider yourself very lucky. If you try to introduce salamanders to the pond yourself, you may find it difficult to keep them. In addition to rocks, they like a habitat that is relatively shady and where there is plenty of leaf mold under which they can hide.

NEWTS (*Salamandridae*)

Newts have laterally compressed paddlelike tails. They live in water at least part of their life cycle and always during their breeding periods. For this reason, newts may make a more likely inhabitant in the pond than salamanders.

Snakes

There is a chance that Water Snakes or Garter Snakes may find their way to your garden pond, especially if it is large and your home is located near the woods or other natural habitat. Snakes can effectively clean your pond of all ornamental fish, and most people do not welcome them to their pond. If you should find a snake in your pond, you can attempt to capture it and relocate it or you can exterminate it. Snakes are easiest to catch in the morning when they are still sluggish from the chill of the night. They are also easy to catch after they have eaten a large meal. For Garter Snakes and nonvenomous Water Snakes, you can simply pick them up by the back of the head or, if you're among the squeamish, you can use long-handled tongs to pick the snake up and place it into a burlap bag. Transport and release it several miles from your home. If you choose to exterminate it, a quick blow to the head with a hoe or shovel will effectively do the job.

In the southern part of the United States, the Water Moccasin (*Agkistrodon piscivorous*), also known as the Cottonmouth, may take up residence in your garden pond. A bite from these venomous snakes is extremely dangerous, and they are not to be dealt with by anyone not experienced in the handling of venomous snakes. If you should find that a venomous snake has invaded your pond, call a local university and talk to someone in the herpetology department. They will be able to help you find a qualified herpetologist to eradicate the snake.

Crustaceans

SNAILS

Snails in the pond do not really benefit or detract from the pond's ecological balance, unless, of course, you have too many of them. They are interesting to watch, and children, in particular, love to net them and observe them in plastic jars and containers. There are many varieties of snails. Some snails are prolific breeders and will quickly overpopulate your pond.

Trapdoor Snails (Viviparus malleatus)

One of the best varieties for the garden pond is the Trapdoor Snail, also known as the Black Japanese Snail. They breed in modest numbers, bearing live young rather that laying eggs, and do not eat aquatic plants. This large snail is winter hardy through zone 5, but does not do well in the summer south of zone 8 (see the growing zone chart in chapter 3).

Apple Snails (Ampula)

Apple Snails are tropical snails that will not overwinter in the colder zones. These snails are both quite over-sized and quite interesting. They are egg layers, leaving rose-colored egg masses on the stems of out-of-water foliage. If you do not want the eggs to develop, simply wipe them off the plant and dispose of them.

Other good snail choices are the Ramshorn (*Planorbis corneus*) and the Colombian Ramshorn (*Marisa rotula*).

Almost all of the snails mentioned above are available in albino strains. These are normally yellow or golden in color, and provide interest for the pondkeeper.

> **A HAZARD OF SNAILS**
>
> Snails may carry parasites that could affect fish. For this reason, you may choose not to introduce them or to rid your pond of any uninvited visitors by netting them out and disposing of them.

Should your pond become overrun with snails, you may choose to treat the pond with a dose of Chevreul's Salt. When used in the proper amount, this will be the most effective way to eliminate the snails while not harming fish. You will want to be careful not to use more than the recommended dosage for your water volume. Net out all dead snails, as their decomposition will pollute the water and leave an unpleasant stench.

CLAMS AND MUSSELS

Freshwater clams and mussels need special conditions for which to survive in a garden pond situation. By placing freshwater clams and mussels in containers or trays of fine gravel or sand in the pond bottom, they will feed upon algae and other organic particles that move through their shells. This is a natural form of water filtration. Clams and mussels should not be added to a new pond, as there will be no established food source to sustain them. Wait until the pond is well established—perhaps the second or third year. Clams and mussels may not be readily available in some areas, although you might locate them in pet stores, aquatic supply centers and fish markets. Do not use saltwater species in the garden pond, as they will not survive. Their decaying odor will pollute the water and make it necessary to completely drain the pond. It is not advisable to collect freshwater clams or mussels from the wild as they may carry parasites.

CRAYFISH

Crayfish of any genera should not be put in the garden pond. They are omnivorous and especially destructive of aquatic plants and fry fish.

chapter 7

Creating a Balanced Ecosystem in Your Pond

Once you have built your garden pond and introduced aquatic plant life, fish and some other pond creatures into it, you will be well on your way to developing a balanced ecosystem. What is an ecosystem exactly? An ecosystem is defined as "an ecological community together with its environment, considered as a unit." When the ecological community is in balance, a ecosystem is created.

The "Food Web"

For an ecosystem to be created, a "food web" must be in place. A food web is a series of interconnected food chains through which energy and materials pass within an ecosystem. The food web is separated into two very broad categories: the "grazing" web, which includes algae and all green plants, and the "detrital" web, which begins with organic matter. Each of these webs is made up of individual food chains. In a grazing web, materials typically pass from plants to plant eaters and then to flesh eaters. In a detrital web, materials are passed from plant and animal to bacteria and fungi, then to detrital feeders (such as bacteria) and then to their predators (such as zooplankton).

There are interconnections within food webs. The fungi that decompose in a detrital web may form mushrooms that are then eaten by tortoises, mice, squirrels and the like in a grazing web.

Sometimes an ecosystem is called a "biotope." It is possible for a garden pond to operate as an independent ecosystem (or biotope). To do so it must contain water, plants, fish, amphibians and invertebrates. Once these basic elements are in place, dragonflies, insects, birds and other creatures will join in to feed and to pass food, creating a food chain on which all participants will thrive.

As part of a balanced ecosystem, fish feed on plankton.

Predators and Prey

In a balanced ecosystem, there must be predators and prey. Plants will be eaten, as well as insects and their larvae, even fish and frogs will become food for other pond dwellers. As dead plant matter and organic waste from fish and other creatures are consumed by bacteria, they create nutrition that algae and basic plant life need to grow. Fish then feed on the plankton and so on. It is part of the food chain.

A healthy ecosystem must remain pollution-free and not become overpopulated by any one species. A good

variety of flowering aquatic plants will help to entice
butterflies and hummingbirds to the water garden, as
will the flowering perennials and annuals you choose
for the terrestrial plantings outside the pond.

Extending the Ecosystem Beyond the Water's Edge

Plantings that attract butterflies, birds and other garden life will extend the ecosystem to include your
entire garden. All living creatures need food and shelter. These are the basics of survival. Individual species
then need additional elements to make your garden
inviting to them. By understanding what certain creatures need or crave, you can make a plan to entice
them. Flowering perennials are wonderful for attracting pollinating insects, butterflies and even hummingbirds. In addition, when planted in groupings, they
provide adequate shelter and security from harsh
weather and predators. Trees, shrubs, ornamental
grasses, flowering annuals and herbs are all wonderful
additions in helping to promote a strong ecosystem.

There are many wonderful choices for plantings that
will extend the ecosystem beyond the water's edge. You
will need to decide, then make a list of your personal
plant preferences and what type of wildlife you hope to
attract. The presence of water will naturally attract
insects, birds, reptiles, amphibians and a host of small
mammals. Your understanding of what plants and shelter material are necessary for a particular species will
help you to draw that species to your garden gate.

Landscaping the Pond

Perhaps you are installing (or have installed) your
pond to fit within your existing landscape. If this is
the case, further landscaping will probably be minimal.
Once the pond is in place, however, you may find
that you have a different view or perspective of your
garden or landscape. Landscape or hardscape tech-
niques and features that do not really accent the pond
may become apparent to you now. You may decide
that a particular tree looks out of place, or ponder,

"Wouldn't an Azalea look nice here?" You may find yourself slowly giving your landscape a little "face-lift" as you begin a journey to bring all of your garden features into a pleasing collaboration!

Trees, Shrubs and Flowering Perennials

Almost without exception, the garden pond will be the focal point and the crowning touch of your garden. The right plantings outside the perimeter of the pond will help to enhance the pond all the more. You will want to keep it lush and beautiful, yet uncluttered, as too many plants would diminish the pond's beauty.

The plants you choose will be dependent on what part of the country you live in. For example, if you live in southern Arizona, you might want to use flowering annuals, cacti and succulents, whereas, if you live in southern Florida, you will choose tropical plants, such as palm and fern varieties.

Tree branches should never hang over the pond. Too much shade could inhibit the growth and blooming of your aquatic plants. The branches can, moreover, fill the pond with debris from leaves, pollen and spent blossoms. Roosting birds can also leave a mess behind.

Before you buy plants for the area around your garden pond, take

> **AIM FOR VARIETY IN YOUR GARDEN**
>
> When choosing terrestrial plants to complement your garden pond, you will want to keep their blooming seasons and coloration in mind. Try to combine your plantings so that something is always in bloom. For example, do not choose all summer blooming plants. Mix spring, summer and fall blooming varieties for long-lasting color and texture. Also, try to combine complementary colors, forms and textures. Don't forget spring flowering bulbs for an early burst of spring color!

some time to study the area. Notice where the sun comes up and goes down. Does the house or another building shade the pond during a part of the day? Are there shady areas where only shade plants will thrive? Is there a rocky area? What is the condition of the soil? When you have carefully evaluated the site, sketch out a plan for including additional plants. You may decide to remove existing plants to meet your new design.

Care
and
Maintenance

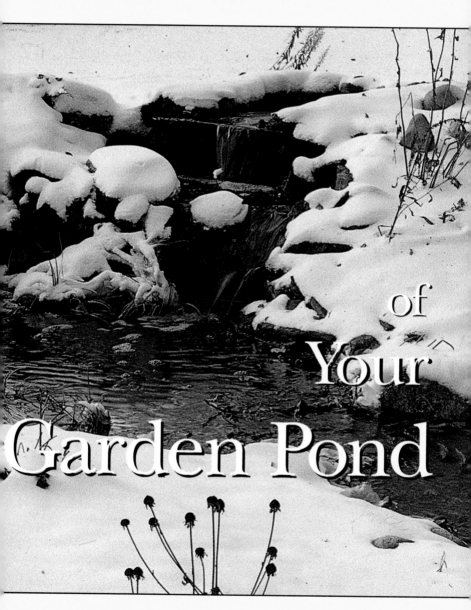

of
Your
Garden Pond

chapter 8

General
Maintenance
and
Troubleshooting

Once your garden pond is in place and operating efficiently and your plants, fish and pond life have all adapted, it will be time to think about ongoing care and periodic maintenance. This can be an enjoyable task—one that connects you with the garden pond and helps you to gain a strong understanding of what makes it work.

A garden pond needs very little maintenance, especially when it has been established. You may find yourself looking for things to do! If the water quality is good and the pump and filtration system are in good working order, the pond will thrive.

The most important rule to remember is that you must keep the pond *clean* and *free of debris and pollutants*, while maintaining a *healthy oxygen level*. When the filter is dirty, you must remember to clean it.

The filter pads can easily be hosed off and returned to the pond within a few minutes. The pump should also be checked to be sure it is free of any clogging debris. This also takes just a few minutes. For a total of ten minutes of care each week, your pond should remain healthy and problem-free throughout the growing as well as the dormant seasons. If you have a biofilter in place, you must remember to keep the pump on, as the bacteria in the filter will die if you shut it off. A fall cleaning of the biological filter media is a necessity, and may be required several more times per year, depending on the size of the filter and the volume of water and debris that passes through it.

Water Replacement

Water in a pond evaporates. Fountains and waterfalls tend to speed up the evaporation process. You may find it necessary to "top it up" every few days during especially dry or hot periods during the summer months. You may use a garden hose to add the water occasionally or you may choose to put an automatic fill valve on your pond. These valves can be discreetly hidden in your filtration or skimmer system. They operate on the same principle as the tank on the back of a toilet. They are very convenient and keep the water at a constant level.

pH Checkups

It is advisable to check the pH and ammonia levels in your pond periodically—even if your fish are showing no ill effects. You may even keep a notebook of these checkups in an attempt to discover when and why your pond is showing fluctuating levels.

Maintain a Balanced Fish Load

Be sure that your fish load is not over the recommended 1 inch of fish per square foot of surface water. Too many fish may cause extreme ammonia conditions, which will be detrimental to the health of your fish and other pond life. As your fish grow, you may need to remove some of them so that your fish load is in balance. With time, as your pond naturalizes, you may be able to adjust the 1 inch of fish per 1 square foot ratio to 2 inches of fish per square foot.

Cleaning the Pond

As noted above, removing undesirable material from your pond is a critical housekeeping activity. Even if you meticulously try to keep leaves and other debris from entering your pond, dirt, fine debris and silt will collect on the bottom and shelves of your pond. Pond vacuums are excellent for removing bottom debris from the pond. They use the force of water from a garden hose to pull the debris into a mesh bag, and they are quite effective. They can be found at pond supply dealers or swimming pool dealers. Debris collected from the pond bottom can be used in your garden to feed your plants. Simply hoe it into the soil!

ALGAE

Skim bubbling green algae from the surface of the water.

Keep the algae growth under control. A good filter system, adequate pump and a low to medium load of fish is crucial. Filamentous or string algae should be pulled out of the pond, especially during the growing season.

If bubbling green algae are present, it indicates decaying matter. Bubbling algae should be removed from the pond as this algae will result in a buildup of ammonia. Often you will notice this bubbling green algae in the pots of your marginal plants where decomposing material on top of and within the soil is breaking down into ammonia.

With a new pond, you must practice patience. Almost all new ponds will go through an algae bloom. This can last for several weeks, as the algae feed on the nutrient-rich tap water. It will also take the beneficial bacteria in your pond several weeks to colonize and begin doing their job to aid in water clarification. Bunches of submerged plants will help to clear the water much more quickly.

Troubleshooting

LINERS

Today's liners are very strong and durable. Once a pond is in place and holds water without leaks, it will seldom develop one. Should your liner develop a leak, however, it may be difficult to locate. Finding a leak is generally a process of elimination. If the ground is wet on only one side of the pond or seems to be seeping water from outside the liner, begin your search at that end. If the waterfall seems to be the source, start there. You may need to lower the water volume as you search for the hole. This can be time-consuming, as you will need to search 1 square inch at a time. In the worst case scenario, you will have to remove your plants and fish to temporary quarters while you drain the pond in search of the hole. Once found, however, holes are easily repaired with a special patching kit available from the manufacturer of the liner you purchased.

PESTS

Occasionally, an unwelcome bird or mammal will find its way to your pond. Uninvited guests are typically birds of prey, raccoons and muskrats. Most of the time they are just passing by, and you need not worry about the visitor. There are, however, times when a persistent pest will need to be eradicated.

Birds

Ducks, swans, geese or any other large waterfowl should be not be introduced to an ornamental pond. These birds will eat and disfigure all aquatic plants. They will also muddy and foul the water with their wastes, while leaving unpleasant reminders of their occupation over the rest of your lawn.

Kingfishers, egrets and the great blue heron are all beautiful birds with a hearty appetite for fish. Egrets and herons are wading birds, and ornamental garden ponds are often too deep for them to wade into. If the pond is an out-of-ground pond, however, it will be quite easy for the birds to walk about the sides and spear the fish as they pass by.

Kingfishers perch on rooftops or treetops, zooming in on the pond with keen eyesight. With one swoop, the catch is made.

If you see a bird of prey at your pond, simply scare it away. Chances are it was just passing by and won't take up permanent residence. If it returns, you can put a heron net over your pond in an attempt to frustrate the bird. The nets do not, however, enhance the beauty of the pond.

Raccoons

Raccoons may appear at night looking for a quick meal. Toppled bog and marginal plants and missing fish are evidence that a raccoon has come to call. You can humanely trap it and relocate it several miles away if its visits persist.

Raccoons may look for a meal from your pond.

Cats

Cats are curious, and they are natural hunters. Some cats will not be interested in the pond because they typically do not like water. However, some cats will find the fast-moving fish inside the pond or frogs and toads lounging within the marginal plants, to be simply irresistible. Cats may sit at the pond's edge waiting for a fish to swim near. Cats may try to catch a fish, but most times have limited luck.

Cats may sit at the pond's edge waiting for a fish to swim by.

Muskrats

Muskrats are very destructive, as they dig burrows into the sides of the ponds in which they live in order to raise their kits. They will dig right through liner material, causing severe leaks and liner destruction. Muskrats will eat the tender shoots of Cattails, Rushes and other aquatic plants. They also feed beneath the ice in the winter, sometimes pulling the plants out of their pots to get to the roots. Trapping muskrats may be the only humane way of eradicating them.

Insects

Plant-eating insects can invade and damage aquatic plants. Black Aphids (*Rhopalosipum nymphaeae*) are one of the more common insects to attack aquatic plants. They tend to gather en masse on Water Lily leaves, Lotus buds and other aquatic plants. They are quite easy to see with the naked eye as they are black and seedlike.

The brown or gray China Moth (*Nymphula nymphaeae*) is also called "sandwich man" or "bagman." Its larvae shred the foliage of Water Lily pads and, in doing so, form zizzag-shaped holes in the leaves. The adult moth hatches from clusters of eggs laid under or on the edge of a leaf. They encase themselves between two pieces of Water Lily leaves forming a cocoon, which they use as a boat. In this protective structure, they are relatively safe from fish and dragonfly larvae and can move about and feed with just their heads and front legs protruding. Affected leaves should be removed as soon as the pest is noticed, as there are probably eggs on the underside of the leaves. At this time you should inspect other Water Lily pads for eggs on the underside.

Gentle wiping of plant leaves (tops and bottoms), stems and buds with damp cloths can help keep eggs, larvae and insects at bay. Pruning and discarding affected leaves also helps to keep destructive insect populations in control.

There are many beneficial insects that feed on the larvae and adult insect pests. Do not kill all insects because a few species are dining on your plants. Dragonflies, damselflies, ladybug (ladybird) beetles and a host of other beneficial insects aid in the control of insect pests.

Pesticides should be used only after other methods have been tried and failed and only by removing the affected plant and relocating it to a treatment tub. Once the plant has been treated (according to the manufacturer's recommendations) and the pest eradicated, the plant should be hosed off before it is returned to the pond.

AVOID PESTICIDES

Never use pesticides or insecticides of any type in or around your pond. Fish and aquatic life are most sensitive to them. Chemicals in these products can travel in the air when you are spraying them on your out-of-pond plants. If you must use chemical sprays or powders in the garden, be sure to do so on a calm day and never near the pond.

Keeping
Fish and Plants
Healthy

Fish
MAINTAIN A BALANCED FISH LOAD

Be sure that your fish load is not over the recommended 1 inch of fish per square foot of surface water. Too many fish may cause extreme ammonia conditions that will be detrimental to the health of your fish and other pond life. As your fish grow, you may need to remove some of them so that your fish load is in balance. With time, as your pond naturalizes, you may be able to adjust the 1 inch of fish per 1 foot ratio to 2 inches of fish per square foot.

EXAMINE YOUR FISH FREQUENTLY FOR SIGNS OF ILLNESS

In addition to keeping the fish load in check, you must inspect your fish frequently for signs of parasites, fungus, ulcerations, disease or unusual behavior. Most of the time these maladies can be readily found in a new fish—the importance of quarantining all newly acquired fish for two weeks before adding them to the pond cannot be overstressed. A single sick fish can wipe out your entire population by passing along a

deadly disease or parasite.

If an ill fish is detected, you must net it and put it in a quarantine tank or bucket for appropriate treatment. Once it has recovered, it can be put back into the pond.

Most fish carry pathogens that may not show up as a disease until the

Examine your fish frequently for signs of disease.

fish is stressed. A fish can become stressed by poor handling, sudden temperature changes (which can also cause shock), a water pH that is too high or too low, spawning, lack of oxygen and being shipped from the hatchery to the retailer.

COMMON DISEASES AND PARASITES

There are several common diseases and parasite infestations that may show up in your pond fish, such as ich (or white spot disease), velvet disease, fin rot, anchor worm, fish lice, skin flukes, gill flukes and hole-in-the-side disease (*Aeromonas*).

Ich

Ich (caused by the *Ichthyophtirius multifliis* protozoan parasite) is one of the most common problems in Goldfish. It is a parasite that appears, once it has developed, as tiny saltlike grains on the body of the fish.

Each of these "grains" is actually a cyst caused by a single living microorganism.

When it first attaches itself to the fish, it cannot be seen. It will feed on the fluids drawn from the skin for a few days until it encysts itself, resulting in its grainlike appearance. It may be seen in its early stage on the tail or fins, as these areas of the fish are transparent. After several more days, the encysted parasite falls off and drops to the bottom of the pond. Here it reproduces; and within one day, each cyst has reproduced up to 500 new microorganisms within the cyst.

After a few days, the cyst breaks open to release the new free-swimming parasites into the water. Each one begins its search for a new host. This is the infective stage of the infestation and the only stage that can be controlled with chemicals that will not also kill the host fish. The total life cycle of the ich parasite is less than one week. When water in the pond is above 68°F, the microorganism will not encyst on a host as the water is too warm.

Ich seems to be brought on by a sudden drop in temperature, but can begin by a variety of stressful situations. Ich is treatable, so long as the response to the infestation is rapid. Medications such as malachite green, used for effective eradication of ich, are readily available at pet shops. To be sure all stages of the organism have been effectively destroyed, treatment must persist for at least ten days. The treatment kills the microorganism before it encysts itself under the fish scales. The treatment does not kill the adult parasite; they must be destroyed in their microscopic swarmer cell state.

Anchor Worm

Anchor worms are also external parasites that are quite common in pond Goldfish, but may be seen in other species as well. Anchor worm is actually a larvae of a copepod (rather than a worm). It anchors itself in a fish's muscle and gill tissue. It looks like a whitish wormlike thread, which may reach ¼ inch in length. Anchor worms feed on the body fluids of the fish and eventually destroy the gill and muscle tissue. A chemical called trichlorfon is effective in the treatment of this parasite if it is detected and treated at an early stage.

Fin Rot

Fin rot or tail rot is actually a secondary infection caused by a number of diseases or an injury. The weakened fish becomes susceptible to a specific bacterial infection—the infection's symptom is a whitish line at the edges of torn or injured fins. With the progression of the infection, the fins actually rot away. As the tissue dies, a fungal growth may appear at the site(s) of the dead and dying area(s). Once the fungus has taken hold, the affected area appears fuzzy, puffy or cotton-like. In an otherwise healthy fish, the fins will grow back so long as the fungus has not traveled to the fin base. Treatments are available through retail pet supply stores. Again, early detection, diagnosis and treatment are crucial.

Skin Flukes

Skin flukes are difficult to detect as they are quite small. If the parasite appears on a fish's fins, the fish may exhibit twitching of the fins and tail. If the mouth area is affected, the fish will open and close its mouth and gyrate it, along with the rest of its body, in an attempt to knock the irritants away. There are a number of effective chemical treatments available for skin flukes and other parasitic afflictions.

Fish Lice

A fish louse is a flattened crustacean that is distantly related to copepods. They are usually of the genus *Argulus,* and their eggs are commonly introduced into the pond by frogs and toads. They are quite easy to detect on white fish or white or transparent fins. The greenish-brown parasites attach themselves to fish with suckers, thereby progressively injuring the fish. They live on the surface of the fish and cause serious damage. They also inject a poison into the fish that causes inflammation and bleeding. These wounds provide a route for the introduction of other disease pathogens. A fish that has been attacked by fish lice swims continually in a line while twirling its body, so that it looks like a large piece of twisted rope being pulled through the water. These lice can be eradicated with masoten, which kills the adult lice but not its eggs. In about one month, you may notice infestation again. It is best to use the medication twice at an interval of ten to twelve days.

Ulcerations

"Hole-in-the-side" disease is caused by pathogens from the genus *Aeromonas*. It is the most devastating of all diseases currently found in Koi. There are many types of bacterial pathogens present in the pond. It is usually only when fish become stressed that they become susceptible to bacterial pathogens, and disease ultimately develops. However, extremely virulent strains of bacteria can even kill fish that are not necessarily stressed or ill in any way. Furthermore, fish can become carriers of the disease, which means that even fish that are not showing symptoms of illness may harbor a latent or chronic infection. Red, sore-looking ulcerations are indicators that an *Aeromonas* strain is present. As the disease progresses, the fish will become lethargic, almost motionless and refuse food. The intestine may be filled with bloody, partially digested food, and it may be hemorrhaging internally. Some strains of *Aeromonas* may be treatable with antibiotics. An outbreak of this disease is devastating to both Koi and Goldfish. Because fish pass the pathogen through fecal matter and via the sores themselves, the water in the pond may carry the disease from one fish to another.

"Hole-in-the-side" disease tends to afflict Koi.

Vaccines have been developed and are being used with mixed results. Koi breeders, especially those breeding high-quality Koi, seem to be the strongest advocates of their use. The two most virulent strains found currently are *Aeromonas salmonicida* and *Aeromonas hydrophila,* and great research efforts are being made worldwide to learn more about these strains of the disease and how to control them.

EUTHANASIA

Pond fish are normally quite healthy. They seem to enjoy their outdoor environment, which is reflected in sustained health when given good conditions in which to live. If, however, a fish becomes sick, injured or afflicted with parasites, you will need to determine if treating the fish is the appropriate route, or if you should perform euthanasia on the fish. To humanely euthanize a fish, mix a tablespoon of salt in a quart-size plastic freezer bag of water. For a larger fish, use a gallon-size bag with 2 tablespoons of salt. Put the fish in the bag and place the bag in the freezer overnight. The salt will calm the fish as the body temperature lowers. The fish will simply go to sleep as its metabolism slows.

Plant Maintenance

Like all plants in the garden, aquatic plants need to be pruned and cared for. As a whole, aquatic plants

need very little care, but there are a few things you can do to keep them healthy.

Flowering aquatics, in particular, need to be fertilized in the spring to give them the nutrition they need to bloom to your expectations. A slow-release aquatic plant fertilizer tablet or two should be adequate for the entire growing season. Some tablets are not slow-release formulas and will have to be used once every four to six weeks during spring and summer. Do not fertilize in the fall or winter.

Water Lilies stay beautiful if kept well pruned.

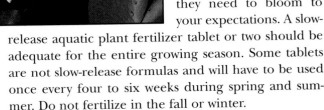

Water Lily pads usually begin to yellow when they have been up for three weeks or so. As they yellow, prune the pad and stem down to the crown. Also remove the spent flowers on Water Lilies. This will help to deter aphids (which are highly attracted to the yellowing leaves) and will prevent decaying matter from polluting your pond. Dead, dying, yellowing or insect-infested leaves or flowers of all aquatic plants should be removed and discarded. Not only will this help the plant to retain its health, it will help to keep your garden pond attractive.

APHID REMOVAL IN A SNAP

To remove aphids from lilies or lily pads, simply spray them off using a garden hose with a flathead sprayer. The aphids will be knocked into the ponds where the appreciative fish will gobble them up!

chapter 10

Seasonal **Care** of Your Garden Pond

Seasonal changes call for special measures of pond care and maintenance. Although not particularly time-consuming, failure to properly practice seasonal care may be detrimental to the health of your pond.

Spring

Spring is a good time to thoroughly clean the garden pond. Remove any debris by netting out the large leaves, twigs and any dead fish. Using a soft brush, scrub the sides of the pond and plant shelves. Check plants to determine which ones may need repotting. Divide and repot cramped plants. This is a good time to fertilize newly potted and established plants using aquatic plant fertilizer tabs. Use the pond vacuum to remove the small particles in the bottom of the pond.

A partial water change is an important springtime activity. Before you do this, draw a bucketful of water from the source you will use to replenish the water that you remove. Test the pH, ammonia level and water hardness. Remove one-third the volume of water from the pond using the pump. Use this water to feed your garden plants, as it is rich in nutrients. Replace the water and dechlorinate. Check fish for signs of illness.

Summer

As plants yellow and die, be sure to remove dead leaves, spent blossoms and other debris. Flowering plants outside the pond may shed petals, pollen and other debris into the pond as well, and these should be removed as soon as you see them. Keep invasive plants, such as Water Clover, Pennywort, Water Hawthorne and Spike Rush, from propagating outside their pots.

Keep invasive plants, such as Water Hawthorne, in check.

Net out any destructive insects and check plants once a week or so for signs of eggs, larvae or adult insect infestation.

If using a non-slow-release fertilizer, be sure to feed the plants once every four to six weeks throughout the summer to keep the plants blooming.

Keep the fish load in check and remove some of the fish if their population becomes too great.

Autumn

PLANTS

As leaves from deciduous trees fall into the pond water, net them out as soon as possible. If you are using a skimmer on your pond, this is a busy time for it, so check the opening of the skimmer and the skimmer bag to prevent clogs from stopping the water flow and your pump. You may wish to put a leaf net over your pond during the fall and winter seasons if leaves are particularly plentiful. Leaves will sink to the bottom of the pond and begin to decay immediately, which could cause serious problems during the winter months to follow. Oak and Maple Tree leaves, as well as Pine Tree needles, produce tannic acid that can turn the water brown and render it toxic. Remember to check the plant pots for leaves and needles as well, and remove them as soon as they are discovered. Dead and decaying leaf matter will show up next spring and summer as bubbling green algae around your marginal plant pots.

Before the first killing frost in the colder climates, remove all tropical plants from the pond and bring them indoors. Parrot Feather, Water Hyacinth and Water Lettuce do not thrive indoors and should be discarded. Taro, Dwarf Papyrusa and Umbrella Palm all make excellent houseplants and can be brought indoors for the winter months. Keep the soil moist throughout the winter. Pennywort makes a wonderful hanging basket plant, provided that a no-hole container is used and the soil is kept moist.

Tropical Water Lilies, Canna, Spider and Bog Lilies may overwinter in your basement or garage, so long as they do not freeze, but are kept at between 45° and 55°F for a few months.

Fish

Early in fall begin feeding a low-protein food specially formulated for Koi and/or pond fish. As the water temperature lowers, fish will begin to refuse food. At this point, stop feeding them as the food will only settle to the bottom and decay.

If you have any Fancy Goldfish or any tropical fish in your pond, you should remove them and overwinter them in an indoor aquarium. Set up the aquarium a week or so before the move. Use water from the pond to fill it. Place the fish to be moved in a plastic bag containing pond water. Float the bag in the aquarium for twenty to thirty minutes to give the fish a chance to acclimate to the temperature in the aquarium. Release them carefully and slowly into the aquarium. Once the fish have been moved, keep an eye on them for any signs of stress, disease or parasites. You will not need to move Fancy Goldfish from the pond if you are located in the more temperate climates where the threat of snow and ice is minimal.

Winter

In the more temperate zones, you will not have to shut your pond down. In zones 8 and 9 (see growing zone chart in chapter 3), where snow and ice are a temporary problem, you can keep the pump and filter system running throughout the winter. If a severe ice storm or snowfall occurs, shut down the pump at the onset of the storm.

Before the first substantial snowfall in the colder zones, you will shut down your pump and filtration system. Clean the pump thor-

Shut down your pump and filtration system before the first significant snowfall.

oughly. Most pumps can be disassembled with a screwdriver. Carefully remove the cover to the impeller and clean it with a soft toothbrush. Remove any fibers, algae or plant particles and carefully reassemble it. Store it in the basement or garage for the winter. Fountain heads should be cleaned and stored with the pump. Filters should be cleaned thoroughly as well. Check all hoses for possible cracks or clogs, and repair as necessary.

You will want to prevent the pond from freezing solid for more than a week at a time. You can accomplish this in two ways:

If snow and ice are not heavy and the temperatures do not consistently fall below 32°F, you may float objects in the pond to help prevent freezing over. An empty gallon milk jug that is filled one-third full with sand or gravel works nicely. A thorough, solid freeze will cause a buildup of toxic gas in the water that will not be able to escape.

As an alternative, you can use a deicer to keep the surface free of ice. Deicers can be found at pond supply stores or farm product outlets (farmers use deicers in their cattle troughs). If your pond is very small, a birdbath deicer may be sufficient.

Never forcibly break the ice in the pond as the impact can harm the fish and amphibians. If a quick thaw is needed and a deicer is not available, try setting a boiling pot of water on top of the ice to melt a hole, which will release the trapped toxic gases in the pond.

> ## WINTER SERENITY
>
> You'll be surprised by how enchanting your pond will be in the winter months. A snow-lined pond provides a venue for quiet reflection. Visit your pond all year-round.

part four

Beyond the Basics

chapter 11

Recommended
Reading

Books

Allison, James. *Water in the Garden*. Morris Plains, N.J.: Tetra Press, 1991.

Arnoux, Jean-Claude. *The Ultimate Water Garden Book*. Newtown, Conn.: The Taunton Press, 1997.

Axelrod, Herbert R. *Designing Your Garden Pond*. Neptune City, N.J.: T.F.H. Publications, Inc., 1997.

————. *Stocking Your Garden Pond*. Neptune City, N.J.: T.F.H. Publications, Inc., 1997.

Dawes, John. *John Dawes's Book of Water Gardens*. Neptune City, N.J.: T.F.H. Publications, Inc., 1989.

Denver Botanic Gardens/Joseph Tomocik. *Water Gardening*. New York: Pantheon Books, Knopf Publishing Group, 1996.

Glattstein, Judy. *Waterscaping*. Pownal, Vermont: Storey Communications, Inc., 1994.

Greenlee, John. *The Encyclopedia of Ornamental Grasses*. Emmaus, Penn.: Rodale Press, 1992.

Grenard, Steve. *Frogs and Toads: An Owner's Guide to a Happy, Healthy Pet*. New York: Howell Book House, 1998.

Matson, Tim. *Earth Ponds*. Woodstock, Vermont: Countryman Press, 1982.

Nash, Helen. *The Complete Pond Builder*. New York: Sterling Publishing Co., Inc., 1996.

————. *The Pond Doctor*. New York: Sterling Publishing Co., Inc., 1994.

Nash, Helen and C. Greg Speichert. *Water Gardening in Containers*. New York: Sterling Publishing Co., Inc., 1996.

Ortho Books. *Creating Japanese Gardens*. San Ramon, Calif.: The Solaris Group, 1989.

————. *Garden Pools & Fountains*. San Ramon, Calif.: The Solaris Group, 1988.

Phillips, Ellen and C. Colston Burrell. *Illustrated Encyclopedia of Perennials*. Emmaus, Penn.: Rodale Press, 1993.

Pritchard, Peter C.H. *Encyclopedia of Turtles*. Neptune City, N.J.: T.F.H. Publications, Inc., 1979.

Reid, George K. *Pond Life*. Racine, Wisc.: Golden Press • Western Publishing Co., 1987.

Riotte, Louise. *Catfish Ponds & Lily Pads: Creating & Enjoying a Family Pond*. Pownal, Vermont: Storey Communications, Inc., 1997.

Robinson, Peter. *Pool and Waterside Gardening*. Portland: The Royal Botanic Gardens in Association with Timber Press, Inc., 1993.

Rothbard, Shmuel. *Koi Breeding*. Neptune, N.J.: T.F.H. Publications, Inc., 1997.

Schimana, Walter. *Garden Ponds for Everyone*. Neptune City, N.J.: T.F.H. Publications, Inc., 1994.

Slocum, Perry D. and Peter Robinson with Frances Perry. *Water Gardening: Water Lilies and Lotuses*. Portland: Timber Press, Inc., 1993.

Spier, Carol. *For Your Garden: Water Gardens*. New York: Michael Friedman Publishing Group, Inc., 1993.

van Sweden, James. *Gardening With Water.* New York: Random House, Inc., 1995.

Waddington, Peter. *Koi Kichi.* Cheshire: Peter Waddington Ltd., 1997.

Wisner, Nancy Cooper and Frederick Albert Simon. *Keeping Koi.* New York: Sterling Publishing Co., Inc., 1996.

Magazines

Koi USA
16023 Placid Dr.
Whittier, CA 90604

Mid-Atlantic Koi
3290 Shaker Ct.
Montclair, VA 22026

PONDKEEPER Magazine
Garden Pond Promotions, Inc.
1000 Whitetail Ct.
Duncansville, PA 16635

Watergardening
49 Boone Village
Zionsville, IN 46077